Dear Chums!
I am in Kazakhstan!

Dear Chums!
I am in Kazakhstan!

TRACY S. SMITH

Order this book online at www.trafford.com
or email orders@trafford.com

Most Trafford titles are also available at major online book retailers.

Printed in the United States of America.

ISBN: 978-1-4669-0660-0 (sc)
ISBN: 978-1-4669-0658-7 (hc)
ISBN: 978-1-4669-0659-4 (e)

Library of Congress Control Number: 2011961732

Trafford rev. 01/09/2012

 www.trafford.com

North America & international
toll-free: 1 888 232 4444 (USA & Canada)
phone: 250 383 6864 ♦ fax: 812 355 4082

For Jon.

For my parents and my closest family (C, K and K)

For my "bezzie" and all my friends!

Dear Janice (my bezzie)

Sitting here on a cold afternoon (apparently it is summer in Aberdeen) and I am thinking about my summer ahead in Aktau, Kazakhstan. 12 weeks away from home, and 12 weeks away from you—more to the point! 12 weeks—3 months—a quarter of a year!

What on earth am I going to do without you, your never ending listening skills and more to the point our champagne sipping afternoons! And what about the numerous occasions when I just nip over to yours after work and have an "impromptu" glass of wine whilst we talk (incessantly, regularly, always . . .) about everything. Most often, our topic of conversation finds its way round to the wonders of men. Or the lack of wonders, mainly.

We have both been married—but for both of us, it's like, well a lifetime ago! We both tend to go through periods of "relationships" although when have we both been in a relationship at the same time? NEVER! Normally it's me sniffling on your shoulder that I am in a relationship "with the wrong guy" (and over the last 12 years I seem to have done that rather a lot) or it's you juggling the advances of several men at once. And my goodness, my friend, how you attract the men? Forget Cameron Diaz, Julia Roberts and Angelina Jolie—I bet they don't have the endless admiration of the opposite sex that you manage to attract! That's because they may have the looks, but they don't have your charm, your big smile and the ability to attract attention propped up on a bar stool that you have!

Do you remember that hilarious evening where you ended up with taxi driver and I ended up with a complete idiot (affectionally referred to as "porno boy") and ended up going for an early morning breakfast (4am) staring at each other as if to say "Who the heck are these people we are having breakfast with?" Apart from you of course who have been by my side for most of the last 8 years or so, keeping me sane through the many evenings of complete insanity.

But . . . . If you had told me 8 years ago, (in fact—even 1 year ago) that I would have even contemplated the life of an "expat wife" anywhere in the world, never mind Kazakhstan, I would have said "Absolutely NO fxxxing way! Not for me".

You, god bless you even went out to Kazakhstan to work for 14 months and seemed to enjoy it—but that's different. You were working. You had a "raison d'etre" other than accompanying a man! You were pursuing your own career.

(And boy did I miss you when you weren't about.) You are always there. Always available for a good natter on the phone, for a cup of coffee, for a moan, a laugh, a chat, more moaning, lots of laughs, plenty of analysis of men and above all—you are always good for a glass of champagne! (or several, because you and I rarely stop at a glass! Who am I kidding—you and I rarely stop at a bottle!)

And now here's me—who 1 year ago was firmly committed to being single for ever more, firmly having given up on the slightest possibility of there being anyone of the opposite sex out there that could ever satisfy all my hopes, needs and desires.

Not that I am fussy of course! No, I think I am pretty easy to please!!

OK, rewind. Perhaps not. I just know what I want, and that list includes:

1) Good sense of humour (read into that—good, twisted, warped sense of humour—and prepared to laugh at all my jokes)
2) Generous (read into that—comfortably well off and happy to share all his hard earned cash on boots—for me! Several pairs required in any given winter—need long boots, ankle boots, snow boots and FMBs—those are "fxxk me boots" in case you had forgotten—a stapler in the wardrobe)
3) Sexy (read into that—tall dark and handsome with a nice body but not too buff—don't want someone that loves his own body more than mine! That just leads to jealousy. Can't have your man loving himself more than you—it's just too, well, weird.)

Those are my 3 top items and really shouldn't be too difficult to find—eh? But apparently so. So, having given up on the whole man thing, a year ago—I met J, whilst in Kazakhstan on business!

So 1 year on, I am now contemplating a summer not just away from you, my family and my other friends but spending 12 weeks—in the same space as a MAN! OMG!

Now you, of all people know I don't have anything against expat wives. Not one bit of it—if you can travel around the world with your husband having a nice all expenses paid life—then I would be the first to say "Go girls!"

In fact, the older I get the more appealing that becomes to me.

And it's not that I have anything against travel or seeing new places.

I have done a lot of travelling over the years. Camp America, as a kid's counsellor, Work America as a "graduand"—the bit of time directly prior to being officially awarded the prestigious title of "graduate" following 4 hard years at University (well, that's rubbish too—I had a ball), and then aged 23 when I headed off on my "round the world trip" which, was slightly cut short due to my lack of funds, and the fact that my friend (sorry Karen) let me down at the last hurdle.

My Mum, god bless her, was quite adamant that my year post graduate working as a "technical librarian"—(literally the most prestigious title I have had in all my working life although I have no idea what it means) would not be wasted, and that I would spend that hard earned cash travelling to the Far East and Australia (as planned) but alone rather than as a two-some.

So, there I was aged 23, a little bit apprehensive (on the inside) but quite unwilling to let anyone else know that I was anything other than brimming with confidence and adventure as I headed off to Bali, via London and Bangkok. The first day or so (to London and then Bangkok) were really quite uneventful. The flight to Bangkok was long, but thankfully back in those days I was not a nervous air passenger as I am today (thank the lord) as to have to wilfully keep the plane in the air for 10 hours whilst contemplating the next 16 weeks away from my friends and family, on my own, may just have been a step beyond my abilities.

But (and although you didn't know me at the time) you will not be surprised to hear, that on arrival at Bangkok and brimming with 2 days of not being able to speak to anyone (this was prior to the days of mobile phone, pre-texting, pre anything that kept you "connected"), I met a rather charming New Zealander (bloke) at the airport. He was all too happy to spend the next couple of hours at the airport chatting away to me and introduced himself as Robert "the" Bruce Mactavish. (Methinks this man has some Scottish heritage.) We hit it off rather well, and as he was travelling to Bali too insisted that I sit next to him on the plane.

Which I do.

And, we then spend the next few hours talking, laughing . . . . And drinking. A lot. So, caution and wind come to mind at this point. And I am once again confident—from the tipple being consumed, and at some point a few miles above the earth, we snog. In fact I think that in amongst plenty drinking and chatting we snogged quite a lot! (No, I know what you are thinking at this point—I didn't join "the mile high club"—I was confident but not stupid)

—I, unlike most people I know, have quite literally lived my life in reverse (at least when it comes to "sensibleness". As a teenager I was quite literally the **most** sensible person in the crowd (well nearly, I was not totally square), rarely if ever giving in to the advances of the opposite sex—which to be fair was rare in those days anyway so choice was not abundant, but quite definitely availing myself of the skills and infinite knowledge of my more "experienced" friends to ward off evil.

I remember one particular event when at last someone did look in my direction. I remember him only now as one-eyed Alex (not a new nickname for the man's dangly bit, although I have to admit it does have a certain ring to it) but quite literally a boy called Alex with one eye, whom at 19 I was told (by Vicky) at the time would be "only after one thing" and for me, aged 16 was a step too far. So Alex was duly warned off before as much as a snog and my teens remained quite frankly as little bit dull and a tad boring (at least in the boyfriend stakes) but extremely safe.

And my 20s were reasonably sensible too—apart from this particular episode on the flight to Bangkok—where, getting drunk with a stranger en route to a place I have never been before, without a mobile phone or any way to contact friends or family was probably not the **most** sensible moment of my life.

But I do arrive in Bangkok in the safety of my "new friend" who insists I stay with him, and am looked after by his "surfer mates" for the duration of my week's stay in Bali! Which I do. Safely (in all senses) and in good hands.

(I did later on in the same trip meet a man in a youth hostel in Brisbane who seemed to have decided I was "wife" material and clung to me like a limpit declaring his undying love—he was also very "experienced" and at 10 years my senior (he was in his 30s! god love him and in those days that was way too experienced for me) having taken a career break from his "lawyering" life to go travelling, did seem extremely worldly and all knowing. He too, took me under his wing, showed me the sights but did, quite clearly want a lot more besides, which became quite apparent when on my departure . . . arranged to meet me in Bangkok some weeks later. I didn't however (I hasten to add) meet him in Bangkok despite my overwhelming desire to have "company" whilst visiting Thailand. But as I say I was still pretty sensible, and sensing trouble ahead decided that alone was best.)

But whilst all these trips have been fun I am a home bird! I like Aberdeen. I like my lifestyle, my friends and family close at hand and the familiarity of our changeable horrible summers.

And you know me better than most. I know you like J—but what are you thinking about me starting out on this expat adventure. What about being away for 12 weeks? Could this be the start of something more permanent?

I have travelled extensively over the years with my job too as you know, and pretty much covered every continent. Much of my time has been spent in Western Siberia, Sakhalin, Azerbaijan and Kazakhstan not to mention the odd business trips to Jakarta, the Philippines and Houston so it is not that I am not well travelled or well versed with the ex Soviet and Russian speaking countries.

But going to places on business is quite different from living there. (OK, I know it's only for 12 weeks but good god that is a lifetime is it not? How am I going to escape when I need to? You won't be there to listen if J and I fall out? And we invariably will, won't we? You know me.)

This summer is just not a lifestyle I ever envisaged for myself. Doing lunch, having coffees, drinking gin and tonic in the afternoon (ok, rewind on that one—doing gin and tonic in the afternoon I can DEFINITELY contemplate! In fact, throw in a bottle of champers, a few bellinis and a cheeky mojito and you and I both know that I am actually quite your girl!) But seriously, it is one thing to do that for a "girls weekend" away—quite another to contemplate a whole life around it. And what's more, you won't be there!!

What the bloomin' heck is the point of all this time, plenty money to spend on champers and lunches, and no you!?? What on earth am I thinking?

What am I going to do all day long? You know I love reading, I enjoy sunbathing and I like the gym, but what else will I do? I will be doing a bit of remote working too but really, how will I fill my days?

And what's more, I have been single for almost 10 years. Independent and single and not terribly convinced that there really is a "the one"! I will be living 24/7 under the same roof as J!

Well, I know what you think about that. You are absolutely happy being on your own—and so bloody good at it. You are a career girl, an absolute socialite of the first order and probably also wondering what the heck am I doing?

And what am I on about?

I am a career girl. Always was and always will be—or so I thought. Things change don't they?

But you've met J a couple of times and you do think he's good for me—don't you?

J is the proverbial tall, dark handsome man. He is over 6 foot with dark black minstrel "melt away" eyes, and it was those eyes that a year ago got me hooked.

The opportunity to join him in Kazakhstan is upon me, and given that I am now working for myself, I think "what the heck?" Well, the balance between being able to work from home, and live a bit of the expat life, is surely going to give me the best of both worlds?

So, the time is upon me to get ready for my summer adventure and try a taster of being an expat "wife". Off to Aktau, Kazakhstan very soon.

Better get on with some packing. So going to miss you.

Love
T x

Dear Karen (my practical sis in law)

What on earth am I going to pack?

You are always so well dressed wherever you go and whether on holiday or at home? How on earth am I going to get everything into my suitcase that I could possibly need for 12 weeks?

I did get some advice from an extremely well travelled expat wife and friend of mine who tells me she always sends a little box of clothes to wherever her partner is. Her man is in Korea at the moment, and she says this is a great way to contain your excess baggage and ensure you have the required "extras" that will invariably be needed.

I think this might just be a good idea.

In fact, not just a good idea—a likely necessity. Why the hell have I left it to the day before I leave?

Well, think about it?—1 suitcase of summer clothes (for the holiday) followed by 12 weeks in Kazakhstan is just not going to cut the mustard. Well, how can a girl survive all that time on 3 pairs of sandals and a pair of flip flops?!! (Admittedly they are Paul Smith flip flops—more expensive than my entire collection of shorts and t-shirts put together—which come, primarily from George at Asda as you well know—but you always seem to find nice things there! My stuff is well, practical but hardly designer style for a night on the town. And in the end of the day, flip flops are flip flops and unless you come from Paisley—and thus have a pair for every outfit, flip flops have a limited useage!)

I will absolutely have to pack my gym kit which means a pair of trainers taking up well required space where a nice pair of Prada heels could be (yes your daughter, my beautiful niece would love that! She takes great pleasure in telling her friends in front of everyone that her Auntie is wearing Prada shoes! Would be good if it wasn't for the fact that 1) I can't really afford it and 2) the rest of my clothes come a sorry second) . . . and like it or not, I will have to have my trainers to ensure my gym routine is kept well in order. Crazy, perhaps but I am sure it will be a decadent period, and therefore, I will have to manage the "excesses" with some kind of "pounding of the treadmill." Yeugh.

Additionally, I can't possible leave too much to chance on the cosmetics front either—well I am just not convinced that I would easily be able to avail myself of my Clarins collection of cleansers, toners, face creams and lipsticks in Kazakhstan (and I am not getting any younger (as you like to remind me being 3 years my junior and not yet reached that middle aged number of 40—so one has to take heed of "age defying" potions, lotions and night creams not to mention eye gels and face masks!) There is no way I can contemplate 12 weeks without the required daily routine of slapping on the face cream to iron out the wrinkles acquired (sometimes in geometric type accuracy) after a heavy night of wine sipping or gin scoofing and a few cheeky cigarettes on the balcony. So, they will have to be packed!

Therefore, 3 pairs of sandals, an outfit for a wedding (including a pair of shoes that will most probably only be worn once), the required potions and lotions (and actually, the minimum amount of shampoo and hair product), the suitcase is now looking pretty full. And I haven't even started packing the clothes!

Thankfully, and this is where your amazing practicality comes in so useful, remember those little Kleeneze bags you gave me?

I adore you for your amazing "monica style" cleanliness and the very fact you have turned my brother (god only knows how you managed this) into a man who is quite house proud. Well, housetrained at least! You are so bloody practical—always have some new gadget in your beautiful kitchen and I love you for it.

Me on the other hand—Practical I am, but although I may well have heard of Kleeneze, I just thought it was that little magazine that people get through the door, flick through once and then put back on the doorstep a couple of days later to be picked up! I never really read it coz as you know I don't really do "housey" things.

Pretty disinterested in cooking (although I guess I can do it if forced) and living in my compact but bijoux 1-bedroomed apartment with minimum storage space, and a hectic social life—what would I need with such gadgets? (A social life that requires to go out at least 4 times a week so cooking can be kept to a minimum.)

Why indeed would I need plastic pegs to seal bags of food in the fridge when I don't cook and therefore won't ever have leftovers!? Or plastic Tupperware containers for the exact same reason. Or pans . . . or . . . .

But you apparently have found some gems within the Kleeneze magazine.

Gems, indeed.

That little set of see-through plastic bags (Yeah they are nothing to look at) have saved my life. Those little see through bags (quite innocuous to look at are quite literally the "dogs bollocks.") These little plastic bags with their plastic zip suck the life out of your clothes and your big bulky big clothes are minimised to a fraction of their former beings, and all of a sudden fit into a tiny space in the suitcase.

God, I love you! And your practical head.

Seriously—I have just emptied an entire drawer full of tops, shorts, cropped trousers and dresses and have reduced them to a fraction of their drawer size and now they fit into the zip pocket in my suitcase normally reserved for 1 single lonesome beach towel! You have no idea how delighted I am with this whole packing experience. It is totally new to me! My clothes are now the size of a hankie!

So, the packing is now going really rather well. My pants, dresses, shorts, tops and bikinis are all squished away into nothing in their little bags, and my suitcase is full! Brilliant!! (Note of helpful advice for you as we both are rather well endowed in the bosom area—these bags DO NOT WORK with underwired bras! So don't bother trying. They just don't roll, and are quite happy being left the size they started! Thanks very much.)

But nonetheless I am quite frankly "Chuffed".

Thanks so much for those little bags!

Love Tracy

Dear Laura
(ex office mate and bridesmaid first time round)

Well I have more or less packed now. Well I have packed the summer clothes!

Fine for holidaying on the beach, but what if I get asked to do some work whilst in Kazakhstan?—well, I might do—anything is possible and after all it was on a business trip out there I met J in the first instance!—I will need a couple of "workie type dresses", and with said dresses, comes a pair of shoes or 2.—and what about more gym kit? There is no bloody way I can survive the entire 12 weeks with 1 gym outfit! Apart from looking like a saddo that only owns 1 outfit, it means washing it daily, and that is going to be far too much effort.

And what about coming home? It will be mid September, and even if the weather in Aberdeen is unusually warm for September, the shorts and t-shirt combo with a pair of flip flops would just be silly. (No I am not from Paisley or anywhere in the general West Coast direction unlike yourself where flip flops are a part of the Saturday night "going out" attire!) I intend to come off that plane looking tanned and gorgeous and not like someone that has just been to Benidorm on a 2 week holiday from Essex. Sorry.

And, above and beyond any of the aforementioned practicalities, I will just get bored of wearing the same holiday gear for 12 weeks. Fine for a bit, but what if you just want to dress up of an evening and all you have is a pair of white shorts and sparkly top? Its just not going to do it is it now!?

So, I am going to take the advice of my expat friend and pack a box for sending to Kazakhstan.

Surely my brother will have a box?! He doesn't throw too much away so I reckon he will have a box. I call him, bless his heart, but after raking his garage (god knows how long that took as it is a bit of bombsite) he couldn't find a box. (That does not necessarily mean there was not a box there, just means he couldn't find one!) Remember the days when you used to get crisps in boxes? I used to think all my Christmases had come at once if ever (which was rare) one or other of my parents arrived home with a whole box full of individual packets of crisps! (It normally happened after a trip to the Cash'n'carry whilst my Dad was buying goodies for the cricket club—I think.) Crisp heaven that was. Day upon glorious day of eating crisp after crisp after delightful crunchy tasty crisp!

Anyway, I digress. Boxes are a thing of the past. He has no box and I have no idea who else to call—as my parents are away and I am leaving tomorrow! Need another plan.

So, I just stuff (well I am sort of folding my clothes) into plastic bags and then put a couple of strong layers of brown paper around them with plenty industrial sellotape ready for sending.

Being a clever girl, I am thinking somewhat cleverly at this point—not in a smart arse kind of way, although, you know at times, I admit I do have an element of that trait within me, that I can send the items to the office of the Company that J works for out in Kaz. Well, I am practically still an employee of the Company too, so don't you think that is a stroke of pure genius? (In fact, I am really feeling quite pleased with myself—even smug.)

I reckon it is the best way to ensure the clothes get to Kazakhstan and the required address—and to add "cleverness" to the whole scenario I have just been to the office, got V to get me letter head paper and stuck that on the front. It has the logo, the address in English and Russian—it cannot fail but get to its destination—can it?

So, I am all set to send the items. Now, I all I need to do is take them to the courier.

The trip to the Company office (based in Dyce) is circa 10 miles from the centre where I live—a little bit of a trek on my last day. However the Courier company is based in Dyce so after sticking on the letter heads, and doing a little bit of "diy blue petering" all is well and time is going according to plan . . . .

Off I go to the courier company, and just before I enter, I go into my handbag for my wallet, to find IT IS NOT THERE. I have bloomin' well forgotten my wallet. AAARGH.

But not to worry, Janice lives not too far away on the North of the City so all is not lost. And the courier company picks up from houses.

Plan B is now in operation and I have a chance of yet another (albeit impromptu) farewell coffee (we have already done the champagne and tearful goodbyes at the weekend), and she is happy to have the parcels picked up and even pay using her credit card. God bless her!

So I arrive at hers and call the courier company. First question . . . "How much do the items weigh?" EHHHHH?! No idea!

And Janice has no scales. And I have absolutely no clue what the items weigh. We look at each other blankly head for the cupboards, and start using bags of sugar to guess what the items weigh. A few bags of sugar seem about the same as this parcel . . . but it is not very accurate.

No pick up without weight so no pick up! AARGH again.

Well, I have the required coffee and last face to face chat for a while with my bezzie, and another big round of bozies (hugs) so there is nothing for it but to make the journey back home across town and pick up my wallet and then head back to the courier with my lovely parcels. The round trip takes about 1 hour door to door—and meanwhile my last full day prior to my 12 weeks away is rapidly diminishing!

But once an idea is in my head, there is no going back. These clothes are going to Kazakhstan come hell or high water, so back home, back to Dyce and in to the courier office.

I am starting to get marginally agitated, and unusually, have just overtaken a rather flash BMW on the road (don't normally bother with such nonsense) but the car and driver were irritating me—they were in my way and I am on a mission!

Excellent. I have got there. Sure, it has taken 3 hours instead of the initial allotted time of 1, but hey, I am chilled, and my plan to send my clothes to Kazakhstan is still moving forward.

So, I arrive at the courier's office with my beautifully packed, in brown paper, with the company logo and address carefully sellotaped to the front and think it should all be all rather simple. The response . . .

"Well madam." God I hate being referred to as "madam"—its just so, well OLD! And Formal! And adding a "well" in front of it just doesn't bode well for what is going to come next.

"Well madam—You will have to itemise all that is within" (your beautifully packed brown paper parcels) "and then you will have to put them into one of **our** boxes" . . . .

Having ripped your beautifully packed parcels to shreds with the carefully sellotaped logo and address on the front.
AAAAAAARRRRRRRRRRGGGGGGGGGGGGGHHHHH HHHHHHHHHH!

OK, my patience is starting to wear thin, but my last 3 hours of misfortune are hardly his fault so I remain relatively cool. So clothing itemised (I ditch a few things for good measure) to ensure they will fit into the medium sized box at a cool £75 and list all the items, giving them all a realistic but a complete "guess" price tag.

(My clothes vary dramatically in price as you well know. I am a girl that likes the finer things in life and I am partial to the odd designer item or 2—again as you know. Equally, however I am not averse to a few well chosen items from the high street or Asda where it is required—so the variety of clothing "worth" is quite variable to say the least. 5 items worth a tenner and 1 worth—at new, 3 years ago, £250!)

Anyway, all done, all re-packed (and I **insist** that the company logo and address on the front is re-sellotaped onto the box), payment made and all done. Excellent, I think—OK, I have now wasted circa 4 hours of my last day but the job is done and the clothes will be waiting for me in Kazakhstan when our holiday to Crete adventure is done.

Excellent.

I remain chuffed with my plan and my packing, and my few well chosen "extras" that will be awaiting for me on my arrival in Kazakhstan having had an extremely wonderful holiday.

Marvellous.

1 week later . . . .

My exceptionally clever idea is slowly panning out to be not such a clever idea.

We are now in Crete, and I have just received a text from my lovely ex-assistant / colleague to say that there is a panic on, and much discussion about a box that the courier company are trying to deliver to the Aktau office in Kazakhstan but the Company (the Company I used to work for, and the Company J **still** works for) would not accept it.

It appears my clothing has been causing quite a lot of E-Mail traffic as everyone is trying to figure out whose box it is, why it is going to the Company office, and who knows about it?
(Currently at this point I am secretly very thankful that I have not packed any sexy underwear! Or worse still that rabbit that you gave me after an Anne Summers party some thousand years ago! Imagine your ex colleagues checking out your spanks or wondering what the electrical item is?! Worse still, what if they unpack the box and hold up my knickers and bras and start guessing sizes? In fact they wouldn't have to do that—they could just look at the labels! And what about the electrical item? OMG, don't know if Anne Summers has made it to Kazakhstan yet, but can you imagine some well meaning but totally naïve Kazakhs checking out the equipment . . . ?)

Unfortunately, the stir has been instigated by charming Kazakhstan customs.

I should have guessed. Not so bloody clever now!

Kazakhstan, now that is independent from Soviet rule likes to acquire money any way it can. Who can blame them really? But they want tens of thousands of tenge to settle the bill and deliver the box!!?

I know my Prada sandals are within but they are 2 years old, slightly worn and besides I could spend a day in London and not spend that!

Alas, several rounds of phone calls over several days, followed by several E-Mails from several internet cafes, followed by several more phonecalls and finally, the decision is made.

The box will just have to go back home!

Excellent! That really had been a clever idea and an extremely really good use of my time (not to mention my money.)

A box of clothes that has made it all the way to Almaty and is now going all the way back to where it came from! Aberdeen.

And it gets better.

The return address is my parent's address (perhaps I did have sixth sense that this might happen) and box finally arrives circa 1 month after it left. At least that bit had gone according to plan.

Well not quite.

Delivery of the box (which originally cost me £75 to send) is now going to cost £297!

Bloody fantastic. A box of clothes has gone half way round the world, never quite making its destination, cost £75 to get there and is now going to cost over 3 times that to send back.

And what's more . . . . I don't have my clothes!!

And neither do my parents.

Because they are retired, and god love them (I don't blame them), are not going to part with 300 squid for a box of clothes they have no need of.

So my clothes have been to Almaty and back, are now currently in courier custody! And will cost me a small fortune to get out on bail.

So, first lesson learnt . . . . **NEVER courier your clothes to Kazakhstan!**

And I am not even in Kazakhstan yet!

P.S. 12 weeks on—There is a happy ending to this story. Thanks to the fact of my Mother's dogged determination and research—the customs on personal items (i.e. clothes you have owned for over 6 months do NOT require to have customs paid)—so forms filled, signed and returned with a credit of £296! Woop woop.

30 September 2011—well travelled clothes in battered courier box are back in my possession.

Dear Dad

Well, we have arrived in Aktau and you would just love this—with your Geography degree and 40 years of teaching Geography at a rather prestigious school in Aberdeen!

Nothing like anywhere I believe you have ever been to in your life—so far (although I do hope you might consider a trip out here—it would fascinate you!) You are such a mine of all information—be it useful or completely and utterly useless (and I am embarrassed and quite horrified to think I used to think you were a bit dull when I was growing up, bless you) but not now, oh no! You are a fascination! The amount of factual information that you have acquired over your 69 years is immense. You devour facts, knowledge and information and quite frankly there is no-one on this planet that would be my "phone a friend" on "Who wants to be a millionaire "before you.

You know everything about Geography—and that includes the finite detail of the intricate road system that leads you to the bottom of any given Munro. Honestly, many an exciting evening have I heard you recount a story of your Munro bagging experiences, and we could be at least half an hour into the story and not even left the car park! Such is your knowledge, your attention to intricate detail and the time you take in telling it!!

(I was told not so long ago that when you drove my brother back from a cricket trip, you managed to talk the entire way home about the same mountain experience! Your poor son managed to fall asleep, wake up and you were still talking about the same trip! And the journey was from York to Aberdeen!)

And I had to laugh not so long ago, when asked about your trip to the cinema. Admittedly you have not been to a cinema in probably over 20 years but when I asked you how the film was (I was genuinely interested in your review of "Tinker Tailor . . ." your response was, ". . . . well . . . . the cinema was fantastic. The seats were so comfortable, and you can see right over everyone's heads, EVEN when they stand up to go to the toilet . . ." (to which I interrupt several times asking you how the film was . . . but you were far too intent on summarising your whole experience from the size of the seats, the temperature of the cinema, the sheer comfort (didn't used to be that comfortable in your day, right through to the colour of the seats and the number of people in the cinema.) Bless you. I am still not sure how the film was.

You also know a thing or 2 about history—the wars are a particular specialist subject of yours, and boy, do you know a thing or 2.

Granted, we would be slightly stuffed if the "Millionaire" question was anything related to music because not only are you completely and utterly tone deaf but unless the subject matter touched on any of the following

1) The Seekers (OMG, I just remembered them!—growing up with "Georgy girl" "I'll never find another you" "The carnival is over" Fabulous! Do you still have the lps?)

2) Nana Maskouri—many a holiday driving to the south of France while that lady with the oversized ridiculous looking spectacles was crooning away (I can't however remember a single track that she did sing now)

3) Charles Aznavour—He was that French singer. I never understood a word he was singing about—apart from "amour" about which he sang a lot—he sounded so "suave" and quite frankly "sexy"—I was a wee bit young to really understand it all, but it really got us into the

mood of the whole French holiday thing. I have a lot to be thankful to Charlie for. Many words from his songs put me in good stead for the young French suitors that would eventually come my way as a young hormonal teenager. "Je t'aime" was one they used a lot!

4) Julie Felix—Going to the Zoo. I loved that song. And have you seen the black and white video on You tube set in the 1960s? Well I suspect not! You, despite your infinite knowledge will most probably have no clue what You tube is! But it is hilarious. And you have to watch it!

There she is aged about 20 singing with her acoustic guitar to an audience of the most robotic, disinterested, bored looking people I have ever seen? Even when they start singing! Seriously, you have to watch it!—it is hilarious. I bet your classroom of hormonal teenage male geography students would have looked more interested in "meandering rivers" than this poor audience!

And what's more you have to listen very carefully. It sounds a little bit like the elephant 's "stiffen up the penis" as opposed to "sniffin up the peanuts!"

Why they wouldn't be interested in that, I don't know!

5) Annie Lennox—anything and all. You have a fair collection of Annie Lennox cassettes in your old MG. And you really are quite a fan. Well of course you are! She is from Aberdeen, and believe it or not—you may not know this, but Annie, I believe used to play in the same orchestra as my Geography teacher and your colleague—Mrs W! Yeah—I remember her telling us that once!

But that, I think is about the extent of your musical taste and knowledge?! So, yes you are a mine of all information, apart from music.

Anyway I have been busy acquiring a few interesting facts of my own.

Aktau where we are living in Kazakhstan apparently dates back to the ancient tribes of the Schythians. However Aktau was founded in 1961 as a settlement, Guriyev-20 when development of Uranium was started. By 1963 the city was founded and at that time was known as Shevchenko. Apparently it was aptly named after a Ukranian poet who was exiled to the wilderness that was and still is Aktau because of his political views, and that name remained until Kazakhstan regained its independence from Soviet rule in 1991.

Aktau (Aktay) is the site of a nuclear power station which went online in 1973 and the whole city was built to house people working in the power station. The nuclear power station produced not only plutonium but also provided power for the desalination for supplying fresh water to the city.

Seriously, Dad on first sight, that is about the extent of it!

You know I have been here on 2 previous business visits (you always love to ask me so many questions and I always fail to impress because I forget to look around or ask questions), I had not really ever stopped to look at it before.

I think I was quick to dismiss its architecture as simply "soviet style"—a city that has no street names and is simply referred to in terms of "micro districts" or micro "regions".

But I am starting to think like you. (OK, maybe not. That would be quite frankly impossible. I have no idea the way your mind operates. It is intense, knowledgeable always thinking about solving the next problem, puzzle or whatever it may be. Could be anything from painting a bench at the cricket club to putting in an electric score board—won't mention that little episode when only weeks after conquering all the Munros in Scotland you managed to come tumbling out the front of the scorebox and give us all quite a bloomin scare!)

But you remain a busy man. Retired now and always busy with some project or another. Much to Mum's frustration at times, you normally have so many "projects" on-going that nothing ever seems to get finished! But that's just you—painting the outside patio furniture, hacking down trees, mowing the lawn, repairing the "summer house", or doing endless "jobs" at the cricket club! The cricket club certainly gets the best of you—and for many club members you are an institution, a man that went in with the foundations as well as the font of all knowledge—whether that be about the history of the club or the drainage system under the wicket—you are the man to ask! (Poor Sheila Murray always requested NOT to have to sit next to you at a dinner party on the concern that she might have to listen to endless and very intricate details on the "drains" at Mannofield. What you could have to say on the subject is simply beyond the ordinary mind—but your mind is anything but ordinary.)

Anyway back to Aktau which on first sight appears just to be a place that is happy to be built around a power station with nameless streets to match the vast amount of nameless and very "samey" type soviet style housing blocks. On first glance these apartment blocks are "nae very bonny". Washing hangs out on the rather sorry looking balconies and the children play on metal bars on compacted dry earthy sand. But they do play regularly and often and there is always a cheery sound of happy children playing on their playgrounds.

When you come from the UK like us, with the history and architecture that we are used to, it is so easy to dismiss many of the buildings as "ugly." (I have to admit I did that so often in the past.)

Much like how I remember Baku (Azerbaijan) some 16 years ago when I first visited it, there are still a fair number of run down Ladas on the road. And god forbid they ever leave the roads!

They sort of "belong" here. This is quite definitely my taxi of choice here! I don't feel right getting into a larger saloon car with comfortable seat covers. Not here! I feel much more "at home" jumping into a Lada with a chipped windscreen, the original seat covers with a few holes in, the back windows rolled down (mainly because they are stuck!) and something I experienced the other day—a sticker saying "GT SPORT LADA"—cool or what! The taxi driver certainly thought he was in a rally car, as he sought to get me to the gym in record time—flying over the sleeping policemen (of which there are many on the main streets, normally prior to a zebra crossing), screeching to a halt regularly behind stationary vehicles—there are quite a few traffic lights here too—on the road to the gym. J tells me there are 3 on that particular main road—and like you, he hates them! You have always been a wonder in the car! Always vocal at the injustice of being stopped, once again at a red traffic light! It is simply not fair—when you want to get somewhere quickly! How often have I heard you curse the fact that once again you got the red light!?

The taxis (if that is what you can call them—you are never really sure if you are actually getting into a taxi or just jumping in to the car of some well meaning local who is happy to take you from A to B for a very cheap 200 tenge-80p) vary considerably on the inside from being clean—often spotlessly with many a different array of seat covers, to being filthy and riddled with holes. The seat covers vary from those knobbly things that are supposed to be good for your posture, through to fur in various colours, colourful seat covers through to "holey" blankets. A genuine taxi here, (?) or all of the ones that I have travelled in, are generally well kept inside in terms of being clean and smelling fresh. The décor often leaves a little to be desired but there is often something interesting hanging from the front mirror. Everything from a swinging Elvis through to dream catchers, Manchester United stickers and other such things.

It is the outside of the car that often leaves more to be desired as the paintwork is normally chipped, there tends to be a bump somewhere, and the fenders or wing mirrors are often broken or dislodged in some way. But to be honest, I rather like it all.

Unfortunately, the Ladas are reducing in number.
Like so many of these former Soviet places, the wealth is seeping through be it corruptly or otherwise, and you see a lot of 4-wheel drives, BMWs and I even saw a red Ferrari the other day!

You also see horses! A lot! People just head riding along, crossing the zebra crossings on horseback. I am unsure where they are off to? A little shopping trip perhaps . . . on their horse.

Apparently, it has even been known to see the odd camel in town! Not often, I hasten to add, and sadly not a sight I have witnessed but J has!
And on the 1 hour journey to J's work site, camels are common place!

It is actually all rather nice.

More soon!

P.S. Kazakhstan has got "real" weather! Proper, predictable weather. Honestly, you know from one day to the next what it is going to be like. Sunny and hot. And when a front comes over, it is also predictable. A few days of cloud and a spot of rain and back to sun! Not like the UK (or Aberdeen) where every weather system possible collides from 4 angles—and gives you . . . . unpredictable, changeable weather! I rather like this endless sunshine.

Dear Mum

Well, I am enjoying the "new apartment" for the first time, which, let me tell you is a stroke of genius on the part of J who bought the place as an empty concrete shell in a brand new building styled on a Dubai type modern block. Honestly!

(6 months ago when I was out here on business, you will remember me standing in the concrete shell wondering why on earth he had ever considered such a venture. Nutcase, I thought. How the hell is he going to get this huge apartment kitted out with all that would be needed . . . ?) Given that this literally started out, on purchase as a concrete shell with a few door ways indicating where the rooms would be. No wiring, no plumbing, no plaster boards, no flooring, no kitchens, no bathrooms no nothing!

But 6 months on, the place has been totally wired, plumbed, plastered, floored, painted, kitchen bought and installed (very tastefully I may add . . . !—Even the lilac walls which I told him several times was a crazy idea—in your presence—who the hell has a lilac kitchen? But it looks really good.)

3 bathroom suites bought and fitted, not to mention "tasteful" beds and sofas and I am not just delighted, but quite frankly, shocked!

And J takes great pleasure on many occasions to point out the Italian door handles that he managed to find. He takes this rather weird "blokeish delight" in not only demonstrating the way that they push down and up (and the whole engineering design within such action)—but just what a work of art they indeed are. (I am slightly dismissive of this whole "pride" thing initially, but having been here a few days now, I am beginning to marvel on the genius of this man.) That said, the whole "up and down" movement of a door handle does start to wear thin after 25 showings . . . . But you will understand this sort of delight having been married to Dad for . . . . ever.

And as to the en-suite in our bedroom—well that is not only enormous but a place to have a party. The shower, which I told you we had decided to model on a Malmaison hotel shower is quite literally a stroke of genius. Granted, he struggled a little with getting the shower heads on the ceiling, but we have a double shower! Yup—2 showers at opposite ends of the shower unit, which is very tastefully tiled and absolutely bloody enormous. You could not only have 2 people showering in it, but a brass band playing in between—and not even get wet! Well their feet would get wet but not their heads! Incredible.) Well done again.

So I am in Aktau in "our" apartment (still getting used to this "our" business) but quite frankly starting to think that I like this guy. Honestly!

Don't buy your hat yet, Mum.

Anyway, the real piece de resistance of the apartment is the balcony. The balcony of the apartment which is on the 13th floor is big. It goes in an L shape around the living / dining area and has enough room to house an outside suite, a barbecue and 2 sunbeds—comfortably. (You would appreciate the whole lying on the balcony scenario.)

And then to the view.

Yes, I have dismissed this city as "ugly" but suddenly I start to see it through new eyes and as I look at out the city every day I see the charm that goes with it. Yes, there are Soviet style blocks, but they have a certain charm and beauty of their own—they are the same, yet different as each little apartment has different windows, broken panes, different finishing and suddenly what I have dismissed as a little ugly and rundown becomes beautiful.

And I can see the whole city day and night from this wonderful balcony.

To the west (?) is the Caspian Sea which is also a beautiful sight and all of a sudden I think that I am really going to enjoy being here.

Indeed!

Dear Jan

Well, we have just had our new table delivered! I use the word "Table" loosely. Whilst it is indeed the table that we did in fact order and a very nice table at that, there is one rather glaring flaw with it . . .

It is now in fact 2 tables. Not 2 complete tables but 1 table delivered in 2 halves! 2 halves that are meant to be joined in the middle to make one whole table. The 2 halves are on the floor making the shape "M" and there is no apparent way that anything can sit on this table (nor is it in any way "fixable"). It is quite definitely broken in 2.

It is a wooden table so it is clearly broken. It will not mend. It cannot be glued together (although I am sure if my Dad was faced with this dilemma he would give it a good try!)—but this table is broken, kaput, finished, done—not to be used. Unfortunately.

I look at J and he looks at me.

I am genuinely dismayed and thinking along the following lines:

1) At what point in the proceedings has the table been broken?
2) Did the delivery men break it on the way up to the apartment?
3) Did it break during the journey?
4) Was it in fact broken **prior** to packing it in the van (in which case other people must have been aware of the table's status)?

---

5) Having carried the table up 13 flights of stairs do the delivery men seriously think **we** are not going to notice that the table is broken?
6) Having carried the table up 13 flights of stairs **have they** seriously not noticed that the table is broken?
7) If they **have** noticed, do they expect us to glue it together?
8) Do they seriously think we will **not notice** that our wooden table has arrived in 2 perfectly symmetrical but nevertheless unattached halves?
9) Do they perhaps creatively think this is an artist's impression of a table?
10) Do they think it is actually not a table at all and just a piece of art?
11) Would Archibald's in Aberdeen, Sterling or any reputable furniture shop in the UK even contemplate delivering a broken table?

Whatever question I ask, there really is not a sensible answer.

Whilst all of this is going through my head, and my mouth is wide open yet failing to say anything, J starts to rant!

"The table is broken! We don't want broken table. Take it away."

Our delivery men who are terribly polite seem a little bit upset at first that they will have to take the table away again!! (Well I suppose that means carrying it back down 13 flights of stairs—although to be honest we could give them a hammer, crush it into several more pieces and they can take it down in the lift.)

Nevertheless, the table was taken away, and a couple of days later we re-ordered a new table, but this time requested it to be a slightly darker shade of wood than the 2-piece table previously delivered.

6 weeks pass by and there is no sign of a dining room table, until one day our driver Genadi tells me that the new table has arrived (in the furniture shop) and would I like to go and view it?

I am extremely excited to get dining room furniture and off I go to see the new table. But alas the table looks nothing like the previous table which was, at least the table we had chosen. A light stressed oak wood. This table is practically mahogany in colour, a totally different shape, size and texture of wood and looks nothing like the original table! AAAAARRRRGHHH!

Another little example of the culture we are living in!

I am not only extremely disappointed but slightly frustrated at this turn of events and decide to take the opportunity to calm down and walk round the shop.

As I walk, I notice a glass topped table that looks very nice with seats that fit well with the living room suite and think this is a far better fit for our dining room.

So all is well. I think this table is going to look so much better. Let's hope it comes in one piece!

Love

Dear Bro

Gees—It is hot! Very very hot. I have woken up after a night of sweltering in bed—we were so sure last night that we could handle the heat, and that it was "not that bad." Let me tell you—it is every bit "that bad"—extremely hot, and not ideal with the air conditioning not working.

And despite having in-built air conditioning in the building the AC is definitely not working! Well why would it? It's the middle of the summer and its 50 plus degrees but who needs air con?

I am delighted with the apartment . . . . and the Italian door handles that J keeps demonstrating (ask Mum) . . . . and the amazing shower that we (well he) designed around our experiences of the Malmaison . . . . and the tiles, and even the lilac kitchen.

No—it is all good, and I am happy. (Honestly—I am happy! Can you believe it?)

(I think I am getting used to the 24/7 thing and we are getting on great.)

However, I am just a tad upset that the air conditioning is not working.

And it is hot. Very very hot!

So, we have decided that new additional to the inbuilt not working system air conditioning units will have to be fitted—no matter how ugly they may be!

Whilst this happens we have decided a couple of nights in a hotel somewhere is a good plan.

We could go to the Renaissance for the night? Probably the nicest hotel in the city. There is the Nur Plaza and a couple of other "world" hotels but . . .

J's driver has a better idea.

So, "Stigl" is suggested.

Stigl is a "beach resort" just outside Aktau and this sounds all rather nice to me. I am still in holiday mode, and J is not going back to work for another week, so why the hell not!

I am not at this stage entirely sure what to expect, but "beach resort" suggests something akin to St Tropez or Nice in the South of France or perhaps St Kitts or St Maarten in the Caribbean (OK I am probably fantasizing a bit at this point) or maybe Fuengirola in Spain—does it not? Even if it is like Brighton I know it will be hotter and I couldn't quite picture Aktau having the Blackpool illuminations so it all seems to be pointing in the right direction. And given that even Aberdeen, our wonderful home time has a beach (a beautiful beach by all accounts, but even a proud Aberdonians like us would be pushing it a bit to call Aberdeen Beach a "resort") So with all this in mind I am thinking that "beach resort" could have potential.

Do you remember our holidays as kids? I think the first "beach resort" we ever went to was on the West Coast of Scotland. I doubt you will remember as you were only 1, and I only vaguely remember it. What I do remember is wearing red wellies with matching red raincoat and red hat. And wear these items indeed I did! For the whole week, as it rained . . . . And rained . . . . And rained. And apart from that I remember nothing. But that was it for Mum. Never again were we going to holiday in Scotland. It was France after that from the time you were 2 (and I was 5) right through until I was 17!

And many a fab holiday we had in France. Because at least in the south of France we were guaranteed a holiday of sunshine!

So anyway, off we go to Stigl!.

And, the drive past the beaches is pretty nice.

We are in an ex Soviet Country, and of course the surroundings still have their own "Je ne sais quoi"—that contrast between the old Soviet block buildings that are really quite ugly to look at, but after a time, have a certain charm, and the old power station that looks as though living within a 3 mile radius could render you likely to grow 3 heads, and the camels that just lie down and sleep on the road (thankfully they don't do that too much, but genuinely—they clearly don't care too much that the road runs through vast areas of desert and if only they realised that the desert area is theirs alone—but lying right bang in the middle of the road is genuinely a little bit risky even for a camel . . . One camel was just laid in the middle of the road whilst 2 cars came at him on both sides of the road. He raised his head as if to say "Do you mind?" and then lowered it again and went back to sleep!) and then there are the beaches and the blue sparkling Caspian sea—which is non tidal, clean and generally just shines like thousands of little solitaires in the water!

Really, it is quite beautiful.

So, I am still excited and we arrive at Stigl.

Well it is OK. A tad "tired", but not altogether ugly.

Inside, however is like stepping back 30 years. You would have loved this! A cross between Fawlty Towers and something akin to an old folk's home. (Thankfully it didn't have that smell that old people's homes have—that stale stench of disinfectant and big pots of mushy peas.)

We are shown a couple of potential rooms, spanning a couple of floors. Each floor has its own recreation area with a telly smack in the middle. The inhabitants ignore us completely preferring instead to stare at the TV set as we were shown to our room for the night. And to be fair, the rooms are enormous. And I mean, enormous!

The bed is king size and looks quite small in the corner of the room. The telly is the size of your first ever portable TV—the one that is still in your old room at home! Should we have wanted to watch the telly (which we don't) we might struggle a little. Binoculars to see the screen would be needed!

However, we were here for the air conditioning and the air conditioning works! Allelulia. Actually, this event reminds me of your time back in Australia all those years ago where you managed to get bronchitis sleeping on a wet towel to keep cool!

This air con works rather well and the room is verging on cold.

Anyhow, we head down to the beach! Well, of course! We are at a beach resort—and it is not disappointing. The beach area is lovely, the water warm, pleasant and so inviting, and, as for the sunset, well that is just amazing! Truly beautiful.

We did have some "issues" getting in and out of the water as there is some massive concrete contraption under the sea, but thankfully we are unscathed going in and out of the sea. Unfortunately (as we later discover), the "employee day" that J's team go on to Stigl involves several "incidents" including a very swollen black and cut eye—someone dived and hit the big concrete block, and a cut foot! When management were told of these little occurrences and asked why there was no warning sign—the response was "don't go swimming." Good Kazakh hospitality!

Nevertheless, I am rather delighted. To be sitting anywhere in a bikini at 9pm with a beer in hand and a remarkable sunset is worth it. You would approve, my brother.

But we are hungry, so off we go for some food.

The food area is café—like with white plastic tables and chairs, concrete flooring and a small bar "thingie". Not particularly posh but when it is warm and you are outside with a beer one really cannot complain!

So we decide to order some food.

The menus come along and we look at them, and then look at each other and then start smiling, and then giggling. All in Kazakh. Not even Russian. Kazakh! We ask for English menus (pangaleeski—that's the phonetic word for English in Russian) and needless to say are looked at slightly oddly and most probably (?!) politely told we are off our heads! (Well I don't know if they said that but their looks did!)

So, we decide to order anyway but have no idea what to order as we don't know what is on the menu and nobody speaks English and we don't speak Kazakh and our Russian is sparse. (J actually understands quite a lot of Kazakh—or so his Kazakh team tell me, but that is in the workplace surrounded by 5 female Kazakh administrators who I am sure don't spend their time talking about food!)

Mmmm. Difficult.

I like most food as you know, so generally I am not too fussy. Unlike you who as a child used to take hours over your dinner and move your dinner around the plate until poor Mum removed it in frustration, or simply left you there until even you felt that you had eat a few of those damn peas! You did however take tremendous delight in "mince and tatties" and have compacted it into a sort of sludge with the necessary seasoning (tomato ketchup or sometimes salad cream aka "Bedies sauce" after a teenage next door neighbour whose name was in actual fact, David) you would then squash it onto your plate, compact it so that it looked as though you could turn the plate upside down and it would remain stuck, and then proceeded to make union jack type patterns as you ate it all up!

However unlike you, you also know that like my shoes I do like tasty, classy food. I am not averse to a bit of "stodge" especially after a night out—there is nothing nicer than Burger King on those occasions, but I can't remember ever dining out and actually ordering chips!

I was quite tempted to get up and walk round all the tables, have a good look at what everyone else was eating, (perhaps even try something . . .) and then point to something I liked! Tempted, I really am! But rude, I am not, so I refrain, and after a couple of extremely difficult conversations we manage to order a green salad, some chips, chicken drumsticks with foil on the ends (that comes from seeing a similar dish passing by and not wanting to miss out on something that looks alright we point to it!—Pretty ingenious I think) and some soup!! Chicken noodle soup! (I haven't had that since we used to stay at Granny's! Do you remember that? Chicken noodle soup followed by ambrosia creamed rice! From a tin, no less. Something that Mum thought was ridiculous given that she—Granny had never worked, and our Mum who did work—full time, took great pride in producing, from scratch the best rice pudding in the universe! Well I like it—I seem to remember your favourite desert of choice was custard. Hot creamy—absolutely no lumps, custard.)

So back to our gourmet meal.

Well, the salad arrives first.

A tad disappointing, but nevertheless a salad. It is green. Very green, as it turns out. (Well to be fair we did ask for a green salad.) It consists of cucumber (lots), a few sprigs of parsley, some other greenish plant (not sure what it is actually), some lettuce leaf type things, a couple of onions (not green admittedly)—and oh a few tomatoes—not green either. Yum.

And then comes the chips! I am genuinely rather excited about them as I have not really had chips in a few weeks and I was ready for a bit of fried potato. They look good!

I taste them and am actually so hungry that I don't notice they are cold.

But J does.

And they **are** cold! And whilst I am still quite happy to partake of a few cold chips, J is absolutely not!

So J decides to speak to the waitress and ask for more chips. The conversation goes something like this . . . .

(J pointing at chips)—"Chips cold. Want new ones."

(Waitress smiles sweetly but nevertheless blankly at him.)

(J pointing at chips and then a little louder—why is it that we speak louder and in pigeon English to make ourselves understood?) "Chips cold. You try. Not want cold chips. New ones."

(Still smiling, waitress nods and seems to have understood the louder version of the command) but now thinks we don't want the chips anymore (and turns to depart with the now even colder, cold chips) which we **do actually want**—well we don't want them cold but we DO want them replaced with other ones—or even those ones would be good but HOT! Please.

So waitress goes to take the chips away, and J says

"No no. You feel chips. They cold"—whilst pulling at her arm and waving a chip in the air and asking her to feel it—which eventually she does once it is squashed into her hand (poor girl), but no—she still isn't getting it! Well maybe cold chips are "in" here? (And still she was smiling. Bless her. It must be slightly bewildering this big English man squishing food into her hand.)

So, after several minutes of this fabulous exchange between J and Waitress whilst Waitress is smiling brightly but with no clue what is being said and J's voice is getting louder, I am literally wetting myself (the tears are rolling down my face) and suggesting to him that cold chips are just fine. You would have laughed too. I can just see the look on your face.

But never mess with a man on a mission—he wants hot chips—and hot chips he is going to have!

So, J comes up with the next part of the plan. A phone call to the wonderful Aliya—the girl in the office with the best English, and a quick resume of the terrible tragedy that we were encountering (bless her! It is a Monday evening circa 10 pm and I am sure she really has got better things to do) and we are calling her to translate that our chips are cold!! God bless us—Brits abroad!

But she listens intently to J, who passes the phone to the waitress—and the light goes on in the waitress' still smiling head (goodness only knows what she is thinking throughout this episode) but she is still smiling and 5 minute later the chips return—HOT!

Brilliant.

So we eat our hot chips and our very green salad. Yum yum.

And then comes the soup and then a few minutes after that the chicken joins us (because you always have soup AFTER you have had cold chips) and it is all perfectly pleasant if not a bit odd.

So, we were still chuckling away but enjoying a little cognac with our coffee, and smiling at the ridiculousness of our meal but nonetheless happily content.

And then . . . . we watch out of the corner of our eyes the most **massive** plate of fruits de mer walk past us! Lobster, Crab, shrimps, langoustines . . . . OMG!! J and I like all things fishy. We have just had chips, chicken noodle soup and cucumber! Brilliant! And those Kazakhs over there are going to have the most wonderful plateful of shellfish. Not jealous.

Note to self—Learn some lingo!

Dear Mum and Dad

Going Shopping

Very excited. Today I am going shopping for the first time to start buying things for the new apartment. I haven't been shopping for a few weeks and itching to get spending! You know how it is?

So, J, myself and our driver, Genadi head off to get a few items for the kitchen.

We arrive at what appears on the outside to be a rather nice electrical shop. There is certainly a very good selection of everything from fridges and washing machines to irons and cameras. (I am giggling at the fact that almost every iron has a British plug! Why on earth—when the whole rest of Europe apart from the UK have a 2 pronged plug . . . !?? I guess they must make a packet on adapter plugs!)

Anyway, we pick our items—an iron, an ironing board and a dryer for hanging washing from the downstairs part of the 2-floored store, and before paying, explain that we are going upstairs for more items.

Which we do—it is all pretty simple at this point. We choose a kettle, some sharp knives, pans, glasses etc. and then go to pay . . . !

And this is where the fun begins.

Firstly we are told that we cannot pay for the downstairs items along with the upstairs items.

OK—we can accept that.

Well we don't understand it, but who are we to question it? And besides, we are still on holiday and have plenty of time!

So, we stand in a queue for circa 10 minutes, the cashier totals the bill, on individual "chitties" (bills), by hand, with a calculator in blue ink (it has to be blue apparently) which takes something like another 10 minutes.

Whilst all this is going on I am standing out of the way observing the fact that there are at least 6 other "assistants" behind the desk. It would appear that they cannot be so good at "adding up" because their job seemed to be to sit there and watch, or occasionally put things in plastic bags or move things around the counter, or talk to each other or whatever it is they are doing) whilst the really important person does the SUMS! For everyone. In the queue. Which is now quite long.

(There is a queue of 5 people behind us now and not one of them seems in any way surprised that there are 6 assistants sitting there doing absolutely nothing when they are queuing for a long time to get their chitties added up.)

Anyway, back to the assistant who is still busy adding up on her calculator and once the sums are finally done, on the individual bills I am secretly and obviously thinking that we must be close to payment and sure to be leaving soon.

But that thinking was just ever so slightly premature.

We are now sent to the cashier's desk where said "chitties" (bills) are each stamped . . . . ! Once this is done we are sent back to the original desk (now queueing behind the people that were originally queued behind us!) whilst we wait to pay.

So, J pays the cashier (and master adder upperer) and despite her obvious ability in the arithmetic department she still somehow manages to overcharge us by 8000 tenge! Good grief.

Having paid by credit card, we are slightly worried that getting the money put back onto the credit card could take (at least) another 10 minutes (and life is only so long) and perhaps, more than likely it would go wrong, we would be charged again and who knows how long it could all take . . . !

So, always there to help and having pretty much memorised everything on sale within the store now, I suggest buying a toaster (which we do sort of need . . . although I don't actually eat bread and therefore toast is not often on the menu) and a couple of fridge magnets (which we definitely need!) to make up the money.

So, items paid for and ready to go!

Well . . . not quite. Because, if you are keeping up with this story we still have a few items downstairs that have not been paid for.

So we have to go through exactly the same process to pay for downstairs items—which are "added up" downstairs, but still have to be taken upstairs to the same cashier's desk for the stamping exercise and then taken back downstairs for the final payment!

We are close to finishing at this point, and I am by now standing half way up the stairs (conserving precious energy)—we have been up and down the stairs so many times, I think it might be smart to hedge my bets and stand mid way!

Our Driver and J are standing in the queue for the final payment (I am getting mildly excited at this point as I might actually get to the pool)—but after about 10 mins standing in no man's land on the stairs, I am wondering what the delay is. There is nobody in the queue but nothing is happening!

The delay is—that despite the 4 other people "adding things up" for *other* people behind the counter, **our** "lady of the sums / cashier / adder upperer / calculator operator / calligraphy expert of the numbers variety" or whatever her job description is . . . . has left a note on the counter saying "gone to lunch"—honest to goodness!! I kid you not! That is genuinely what it said.

Once Genadi has translated this to us, we can't help but laugh and decide that we will just "go to lunch" ourselves—so that is what we tell them and that is what we do!

Poor Gena is sent back to settle up later!!

Note to self—allow lots of time when going shopping.

Dear Mum and Dad

Shopping for furniture and other household goods.

Not perturbed at all by last week's shopping experience I am, once again quite excited about the prospect of going shopping.

I have been away from home for about a month now, and have not been shopping for probably over 6 weeks. That is quite a record in my life. No clothes have been bought, no new cosmetics, no new DVDs, no shoes, boots and not even anything pointless that you just buy for the sake of buying something because being a girl, there is always something to buy when money has not been spent for a while!

So, the opportunity to go shopping, safe in the hands of our Driver with absolutely no cap on the money for spending was quite an exciting prospect.

The plan was to buy items for our beautiful but rather sparse apartment.

J, had indeed done a brilliant job of the kitchens, bathroom and even managed to acquire a couple of nice double beds as well as a very nice suite for the living room—so I was quite optimistic about what I could buy with my tenge!

The shopping list of possible items consisted of the following:

Table (for the hall)
White china tableware
Photo frames
A vase or 2

A chaise longue
Light fittings (for the 2 bedrooms, the dining room and the living room)
Blinds for the windows
Sun beds for the balcony
Rugs
Anything else that I see that will make the apartment look homely!

I was excited and sure that by the end of the day, I would have successfully filled some of spaces in our apartment.

The first stop was a shop almost directly across the road from our apartment. A photo shop to buy photo frames. "Good start" I thought, and so we entered what looked like an office with people sitting at desks, answering phones and looking at us like we had 3 heads.

Apparently they don't sell photo frames at all! (Seemed somewhat obvious to me from the outset, but anyway we bussled out of there and were directed 2 doors down to what really was a photo shop.) Aaah!, I thought that this could be more promising, but alas no photo frames there either.

Never mind, I was still upbeat and not upset by the false start.

On to another shop.

This time, it was a furniture shop . . . . I think. In the porch area there was outdoor furniture. A quick glance revealed that unless I wanted a well (yes, a well for getting water out of . . . !?) on the balcony, and a table for 12 then there was not much there that was going to do for our outdoor area (I was looking for 2 wooden sunbeds), so on we went inside.

I have never seen anything like this place. Clearly it is a furniture shop, but the layout gives it the appearance of a warehouse. Sofas hanging from the roof and wardrobes packed in back to back in row after row of wardrobe. All slightly crowded and quite frankly, disturbing. Plenty to choose from, but nothing in the many rows that really "tickled me."

So on to the next shop, and the next shop and the next.

Unlike in the UK, where furniture shops that are not in the centre of a town centre are generally all piled together on an industrial estate, in Aktau, the shops are scattered all over the city. There appears to be no particular reason for why they would be in a particular micro district or area and there is absolutely no indication from the outside of what kind of shop you are entering.

Every time I go to a shop for the first time with Genadi in Aktau it is a surprise as to what I am going into. Even if I could read the sign on the outside of the shop, there often is no sign, and there is never any indication of what kind of shop you are entering. Normally more reminiscent of a warehouse with bars on the windows and no windows at all, I enjoy playing a game with myself trying to guess what shop I am going into.

So, several shops later, and the likelihood of finding "modern" furniture for the hall, or a chaise longue appears to be slipping away from me. The furniture in general reminds me of something out of the "ottoman empire"—it is all very wooden, elaborate and quite dated by my taste.

What is interesting to note, is that every now and again there is a "gem" in amongst it all so patience and perseverance are important to the cause if you are going to succeed at furniture shopping in Aktau.

On to the lighting shops. There is a fair amount to choose from, and whilst my taste initially appears poles apart from Genadi's we do, eventually agree on lighting for the dining and living rooms.

The process of buying the lighting is, as ever a long drawn out and somewhat onerous process. Every single light fitting is taken out of its box—and as the chosen fitting for each room comes in a line of 3 matching frosted glass shades (we intend to hang them in diagonal line from the ceiling running from high to low), they all have to be checked, in the light for any chips or flaws before being re-boxed. This process is extremely frustrating, but nonetheless, thorough.

We go from here to several other bazaars. (Probably should call them "bizarres".)

We are looking for things like vases, photo frames, table china and anything else that I happen to notice that might help finish off the apartment. In between looking at the interesting array of goods, I notice that there are nail bars, and as my toe nails are needing re-painted I ask Gena to stop at one of the nail bars and choose new nail varnish, cotton wool and nail varnish remover! All seems pretty simple.

The shop assistant goes to put my goods into a bag, and Gena goes to pay—but I realise that the nail varnish remover has not been put in the bag. I remind Gena that I need the remover too, and he says something in Russian, to which the apparent reply was "this is not for sale!"

What do you mean it is not for sale?

Apparently the other end of the stall belongs to somebody else and this cannot be sold in her / his absence! Brilliant.

Ok, so I am starting to get weary (we have been shopping for over 4 hours, and I have so far bought light fittings for the living room and dining room and nothing else.)

Anyway this bizarre bazaar has a large number of individual shops selling tableware so I start the hunt for plain white china. There is some very nice white china that I like, but in the first shop it apparently can only be sold as part of a black and white set. Half the plates are black and the other half are white. Not exactly what I am looking for! So we move on to the next shop, and the next, and the next (In between looking for photo frames which we do finally find) and discovering one shop that had one single random glass vase (perfect!) that I also decide to buy—who knows if or when I might ever find another one?

Still no table ware, and Genadi and I have been shopping for almost 5 hours!

I am exhausted, and weary, and decide that I have genuinely had enough for one day.

So we decide to go home.

We do however stop on the way, and Gena suggests one last shop (I am unclear at first what this might be selling given that I still don't have a table for the hall, a chaise longue or chair for the dining room, wooden sunbeds for the balcony, rugs or blinds for the windows!) But it turns out it is a china shop and really quite tasteful too!

I find a set of white china which is square in shape and looks perfect. I am very excited that we may have discovered another gem for the day, and tell Gena that I want to buy it. He duly translates my request to the shop assistant whose response is "Sorry, it is not for sale as it is not a complete set!!!!"

Clearly my thoughts are "so why are you displaying it?" but I am too weary and too tired by this stage to be surprised by this, and decide that I should leave quietly.

So we do.

Another 5 hour shopping afternoon in Aktau, and I have managed to buy 2 light fittings, 3 photo frames and a vase!

But, rather than dwelling on the lack of quantity, I am somewhat delighted at the quality given the choice. My vase will fill another corner and the light fittings look fantastic.

Dear Ali (my wonderfully practical friend who has converted her Granny's apartment from scratch!)

OMG—Well we are living in a new apartment which is fantastic. But in a new build as you can imagine there is a LOT of repair going on. Drilling, hammering, more drilling, banging all day long—it's driving me insane.

When I told J that my head had a drill going through it his initial response was something along the lines of . . . . "Well you just have to put up with it. It's a good sign that lots of people have bought the apartments and folk are moving in."

Sympathy indeed I thought, but I guess I had to agree with him and for days, weeks I have put up with the constant drilling.

Some days it is not too bad. As long as the drilling is one continuous "mmmmmmmmmmmmmmmmmmmmmmmmmmmmmmm" I can deal with it. My biggest frustration is when there is short blasts of "mmmm"! silence! bliss! "mmmmm"! silence! bliss!! "mmmmmmmmmm!" silence! Bliss! until I am humming along with it and shouting at the walls, the floor, the ceiling "aaaaaaaaaaaaaaaaaaaaerrrrrghh!"

Anyway, a little trip out onto the balcony, a cup of coffee and a 10 minute blast of sunshine and I am, once again cool with it and prepared to put up with it.

My biggest laugh came the first Sunday J was home and circa 11am in the morning the drilling started. "mmmmmmmm" and within 5 minutes, the steam is coming out of J's ears and he turns to me and says "Is this what it is normally like?" A little nod from me and J says "I have no idea how you put up with it?"

Yes, indeed I think. Now that it affects him, it is suddenly a different issue.

So J ups out of bed (well it was his Sunday off and he likes a good sleep) and is almost out of the apartment with nothing on (until I remind him that he had better cover up his bits) and off he goes to sort the drillers out!

15 minutes pass and he returns, sweat dripping off his brow and steam still coming out of his ears and tells me he has been to the 14th, 15th, 12th, 10th and 9th floors and can't find where the noise is coming from!! (I am trying not to smile, and feel now is probably not the most opportune moment to ask why he had not gone to the 11th floor . . . ?)

There is only one thing for it, says J—and that is to phone Raya. Raya is our Kazakh friend, colleague and the fix-it woman of Aktau. You want a job done, and Raya is your woman. Not that I am entirely sure this is a good use of her time but J is straight on to the phone to Raya and within 15 minute of the call (less time than it took J to scour the 5 floors) the drilling has stopped!!

Amazing—brilliant!

And we can have a Sunday in peace!

There is, of course several signs throughout the building (written in Kazakh or Russian or something that I certainly can't read) that indicate noise (drilling etc) must be contained to between the hours of 9am and 5pm Mondays to Saturdays but this does not seem to stop the many immigrant workers from banging away at whatever time of the day pleases them.

We have at least 2 other occasions during the summer to phone Raya and get the drilling stopped, which invariably it does—very quickly! Such are her powers!

Everyone needs a local fix it person!

Dear Bro, Sis in law and Toots

Well I bet you are dying to find out what a night out in Aktau is like?

For us, it is certainly not a pub crawl down Union Street. Although Aktau is not large, things still feel spread out to me. The smashing thing about this place is that jumping in to a taxi (I use the term slightly loosely as it is literally impossible to tell what is a taxi and what is not—although a good clue is normally the more run down the car, the more likely you are to get a lift in it!) is an easy and very cheap experience. It is 200 tenge (about 80p) to go anywhere in the city! Brill.

Nevertheless, there are quite a few places to eat out in, although J is quite set in his ways and we limit our restaurant goings to a few favourites such as Taksim. Taksim has a nice outside area as well as the indoor part for the winter and during the summer it is a great place to eat. Towards the end of the summer this year as the evenings started to get a little colder, you get given a blanket. A rather nice touch, I thought until I was eating out with J and 2 of his friends (male) and the 3 of them were clad in leopard skin, lime green and pink blankets! Bless them.

In Taksim, the staple diet for us is chicken fajitas. They are really very nice. (It makes me laugh, however that whilst the chicken is beautifully cooked and very yummy, the accoutrements that come with said dish vary every **single** time you order this dish! Sometimes you get onions, lettuce—which I admit is very hard to come by in Aktau and a salsa dip, other times you may get a guacamole-type dip, but you never ever, unless you specifically request it, get soured cream! And request it, we do, every single time we go!)

There is Pinta just next door that also has quite a good menu and our favourite place for shaslik—the "local" outdoor restaurant with an unpronounceable name. This is a great outside place in the summer as it looks right over the Caspian and the food is excellent. The only downside to this place is the 3 floors of stairs to get to the toilet, which if you are wearing heels is bad enough anyway, but when you get to the top, you find a toilet that reminds me of our early years of holidaying in France where all the toilets were "holes in the ground" that you had to hover over. (Not the most enjoyable experience at the best of times but quite awful when stricken with a bout of diarrhoea you have to hover and squat for what feels like hours and aim . . . ! Awful.) So this place has a hover toilet "on stilts" you actually have to climb onto it once inside the toilet—thus more climbing and a bit of balancing that, in 3 inch wedge sandals and a dress does not conjure up the image of sophistication. Just as well, that to date I have not been too drunk whilst in this particular restaurant because knowing me it is perfectly conceivable that under the influence of too many sherbets slightly unsteady in squat position could certainly render me stuck down a hole with legs flailing in the air! Not a bonny sight!

J and I sometimes avail ourselves of the delights of the Renaissance hotel (where I go to the gym and use the pool 3 or 4 times a week) just to gain a little bit of "international" normality. The beauty of the Renaissance is that you could be anywhere in the world which I admit is something I would never do on holiday, but in Aktau is a "must" from time to time!

I say "normality" in the sense of the décor. In terms of the service, that can be extremely "Kazakh" or is it Soviet in style? Sometimes the service is excellent—quick, attentive, customer focused and interested. (Just what you would expect from an internationally recognisable hotel.) At other times, well it can be quite the opposite. Slow, disinterested, dessert before main course, finished your starter before the wine comes . . . etc. But the food is generally always very good, and a great place to have a nice steak when the mood prevails.

One evening I suggest to J that we should eat out, and that I would like to go somewhere new. He suggests we go to Napoli next to the Nautilus and explains that he has not been there for several years! He says that a few years ago they did a very good Chinese but in recent years it has "gone off" but why don't we give it a try anyway?

I am quite hungry and obviously have not had a Chinese in quite some considerable time, am always willing to try out something different, so off we go.

Somewhat bizarrely as you walk in the door it has the appearance of a Chinese type restaurant but as you look to the left, there is a bowling alley! Weird, I think.

Anyway, J leads me upstairs to what appears to be the Chinese restaurant and we sit down in one very empty restaurant. There are circa 10 tables (all empty) and Chinese pictures on the walls, lanterns on the ceilings and all appears to be rather authentic looking.

The whole place is very dark, and as it is still lovely and warm outside, and the Caspian is directly outside the window, J asks that the window be opened. This lets not only some fresh air in, but brings a small amount of additional light into the very dark, dingy restaurant. It also gives us a small view (we have to move the wooden blinds ourselves and hang them precariously over the window in order to see out as they are, unsurprisingly broken and the pulleys will not work) of the beautiful pink sunset which never ceases to amaze me as the sun literally melts into the Caspian.

J requests that lights are switched on (he can't read the menu because it is literally that dark) but we are told that the lights **ARE ON**, and we realise on closer examination that this is indeed true.

There are 10 lights on the roof (yes I counted them) and of those 10 lights, 7 are not working! One would have to conclude that as the bulbs "blew" they were simply not replaced!

At this point, I am sitting reading the menu and am slightly confused at what I am reading. I know it is dark but the menu appears to be pastas, pizzas and very Italian style dishes and J is still talking about ordering Kung Po chicken!!

I finally ask him if we are reading the same menu, and then realise that in fact, we are not. This Chinese restaurant doubles up as an Italian and we are indeed reading 2 different menus! Interesting. The clue was in the name of the restaurant (Napoli) but given the décor was most definitely Chinese, I could be forgiven for forgetting the name of the restaurant.

Anyway, we are hungry and it is Monday night of a Monday holiday and we order a couple of Chinese main courses. The food is actually rather nice, albeit hard to see as we are, in effect eating in the dark . . . . And on our own as there is not another single person in the restaurant. (Another clue)

There is plenty of people downstairs in the bowling alley—a really odd concept when eating a Chinese meal in a Chinese restaurant but nobody eating with us in the restaurant.

Anyway, J remains convinced that the quality, food and service of this place is not as it was 3 years ago, and vows not to return. I quite enjoy it, and once again put it all down to my experiences of Aktau.

Hilariously, a couple of weeks later once I have met the "expat wives" we meet here at lunchtime and I am told that I have to meet them outside in Napoli!! There is, apparently a beautiful outside eating area looking out over the Caspian through the main restaurant (downstairs) which neither J nor I even knew existed!!

So whilst we were sitting in a run down, probably no longer used dining area, everyone else was probably eating elsewhere!!

I suspect the upstairs area has not been used in many years! But rather than tell us that there was another restaurant area (and an area for a distinctly more aesthetically pleasing eating experience in the sun, outside, looking out onto a beautiful sunset and the calm Caspian sea) we are left to our own devices in the run down, disused former upstairs Chinese restaurant—in the dark!

What is even more hilarious to me is the "eureka moment" in my head as I remember that J has a serious hobby in DISUSED RAILWAY STATIONS. Honestly! This is one of his major hobbies, and I am beginning to understand that his interest and enjoyment and perhaps his ability to overlook the fact that the restaurant we were eating in was not only empty, the chairs and tables had not been used for years, there is an inch of dust on the tables, the bulbs in most of the lights were broken, the blinds were filthy, and the carpet was not only stained but sticky under foot is purely indulging him in his guilty pleasure! It is, of course disused!

Ah well, put it down to another experience. Only we could manage to eat in a disused restaurant . . . . And get served!

Dear Betts

I am slightly annoyed that I have been shipped off to Baku (Azerbaijan) for 4 days—especially as its J's birthday today, and he is playing it down. It's a big birthday too! And I have so many ideas about how we are going to celebrate this big birthday—but no, my visa is running out and my window of opportunity is closing in.

So I am heading to Baku tonight to renew my visa for Kazakhstan.

Don't you think it is a bit odd that whilst you are in Kazakhstan, you have to leave Kazakhstan to go to the Kazakhstan embassy in another country to gain the visa to go back into Kazakhstan—where you are already!?

But them's the rules—so off I go.

The good news is, I get to spend a few days with you my friend.

I have been in Baku many, many times over the last 16 years and it is probably the one place (apart from London) that I have visited the most often on business. In that sense, I feel a sort of affinity to Baku.

Over the years I have worked for 3 different companies, all of whom had and still have a presence within Baku so I am sure to meet some colleagues, ex colleagues, and "others" when I visit. (more on that later . . .)

I have had plenty stories to tell over the years too.

My pal Lindsey was out there for over 10 years running her own Company and how proud I am of her achievements there. Going to Baku back in the late 90s was a treat. She knew the place, I didn't, she had clout and friends and I had someone to "party" with! Fab. And party we did.

The Caledonian Society did a few events and I was lucky enough to be over for a St Andrews do back in 2005.

That was the year I had just returned to Aberdeen to work, and to the Oil and Gas industry after a year (a lifetime) working for a House building company and living in Manchester. Manchester I loved, but the job I did not. And I remember to this day, that my first business trip on return to Oil and Gas was a trip to Baku! Home from home! I swear to god, stepping off that plane (in fact I should have said stepping ON that plane . . . I knew more people heading to and working in Baku than I had ever known in Manchester!)—It really remains true to this day that the only people I even recognised in Manchester were actors from Coronation Street!

So back in 2005 I return to Baku once more and back in the midst of Oil and Gas, with a long weekend to look forward to with my pal, Linz. Funny now, in particular as her friends, Rod (and his wife) is now your boss!—the guy I met umpteen years later, and suggested, that he hire you! (as by this time I am working for the same company as him.)

So there I am back in the day at he St Andrews Ball in amongst so many names and faces that I either knew or half knew, or at least recognised, and quite frankly felt completely in my element.

And . . .

Do you remember hearing about the time when myself and one of your colleagues (Angie) partied until 2 am, went back for an hour's kip and then almost missed our flight? I was green! But managed to hold it together until we landed in Heathrow, where I spewed into a bag just as we hit the runway! She couldn't look at me for fear of throwing up herself and held a pillow between my face and her! And I was her boss! And we were sitting opposite a consultant who was in the office throughout the entire visit—and we both thought was just "one of the locals"! How embarrassing!

And do you remember another such business trip (Sakhalin Island actually) where I was with your best pal and we partied until 4 am—also the night before we were leaving and D decided to have an early breakfast in her room? I remember the phone call the following day when she discovered (a little more sober) that she had emptied the mini bar of its contents, including a couple of beers, a snickers, a twix, a can of peanuts, a box of Pringles and a bounty! D was still discovering the evidence as she called me from her room the next morning circa 11am . . . ? "OH My god . . . I had a feast after I left you . . . . And there's a twix wrapper . . . . and peanuts all over the floor . . . . and there's a bounty wrapper too!!"

This visit, however I am here on holiday and therefore have 4 days of not working—and I am pretty sure plenty of partying.

I am looking forward to seeing you, Betts—possibly the one person over the years who has worked for me, that I have seen make the most change. You have blossomed from Betts (it wasn't me that named you Betts after Ugly Betty) but your work mate and chum who observed your antics and your "style" as being a little bit like the unfortunate Ugly Betty. Bless you—always dressed exceptionally well (and I have to laugh at your 3 double wardrobes—1 in your own room and 2 in mine filled to bursting point with dresses—of every single colour imaginable—you are going to need a 25 foot container just to ship your clothes back when or if you leave) but you used to have this funny trait where something, at some point would end up of falling off your attire, or trailing along the floor or worse still the mud (and you would trip over it), or end up with a broken heel or some such Betts type misfortune.

Personally, I see you (or saw you then) more as a cross between Bridget Jones and Calamity Jane. Someone with a big heart, always a story to tell, sometimes a little awkward in your own skin but just bursting to blossom into the star of the show.

You are kind to the core, but back in the day you were a nervous crater from a small fishing village in Aberdeenshire. You are bright, but used to hide behind your anxiety, and rarely let anyone see the sparkle under the fiery red head (which is there I now know.)

You have blossomed into "confident Betts" and as you told me a couple of years back when explaining your new found confidence "I dinna take beamers nae mare" to proudly explain the fact that the days of the "bright red faced" girl was a thing of the past.

Nope Betts has really gone, thanks to almost 3 years in Baku—and all of them working for me! Well, the first year was, and your current job, I played a small part in getting for you. But I am now your "ex" boss and boy do I know it!

Anyway, my flight across from Aktau to Baku is short—about an hour in duration. And thankfully, I have been out with J and a few of the guys in Aktau so have had a few cognacs prior to take off to help with the nerves. I have become a bit of a panic flyer these days, and find the whole experience of flying a nail biting experience. I have little choice but to **will** the plane to remain in the air (after a few heartfelt prayers), I **will** the pilot to remain alert and have all on board to "flap their wings" in their heads so that we will all stay in the air. At times, I can be counting the seconds that count the minutes to the point where we will be descending into land, and once again my safety. The slightest amount of turbulence and I am hanging (and I mean gripping very tightly) to the person sitting next to me—which on the several occasions when the poor individual is not only a stranger but a stranger who doesn't speak any English, is all in all quite embarrassing.

This is one such flight. I am sitting next to a very small lady (about half my height) with white hair who is sitting with her weekend bag (a rather large holdall) on the floor at her feet (and under my feet too which at the end of my very long legs are struggling to find space to wrap around this rather large bag. Her handbag and her laptop bag are on top of the tray table (which is NOT in the upright position as we have been told to "fold away" prior to take off) for the entire journey—inclusive of take off and landing.

I smile (well grimace actually) when the air attendants take more interest in ensuring that the blinds are up rather than the tray tables up, mobile phones firmly off, and luggage safely tucked away.

My plane mate also has her mobile phone out . . . and **on**, as have the vast majority of all other passengers on the flight so why should she be any different? (and I distinctly remember hearing that mobile phones are meant to be switched off for the **duration** of the flight—I can only presume (hope) that the translation into English is the same as the Russian version . . . but I am beginning to wonder . . . .), as they are **all** texting and phoning away continuously throughout the whole flight! For me, this only adds to my "nervous whilst flying" state and therefore as soon as the propeller plane (not a jet) starts jiggling about, I start to panic (ridiculous I know) . . . . convinced as I am that we are all going down thanks to the fact "her" tray table is down, and everyone's mobile phones have interfered with the plane's navigation system. And what's more the 7 foot man in front of me has decided to recline his seat and his head is basically resting on my lap so I am firmly wedged between 7 foot man, weekend luggage and cuddly white haired lady.

But who cares about my discomfort, the plane is rocky and bumpy and it is all quite vigorous!! And I am in fear for my life. At this point, I grab white haired lady's arm—tightly! (Not entirely sure why I think this will make any difference to our fate, but somehow whilst grabbing tightly and hanging on to this small cuddly little lady I feel somewhat calmer.)

Picture the scene—all 5 foot 9 of me, who initially looks quite cool, calm (and sophisticated—in my head anyway) is hanging on to some 4 foot tall yet round woman with white hair (who may have been Polish, Azeri or Russian—really not sure) for dear life. She smiles at me, pats my hand and gives me . . . . a wet wipe! (bless her—very generous, but what the hell do I need with a wet wipe if I am about to plunge 3000 feet into the Caspian Sea—I will be **very** wet then, and probably very dead?!)

She appears very sweet though, and happy for me to continue clinging (tightly and most probably stopping her circulation) for a few minutes until the jiggling stops—and then she shouts over my head at what I can only assume are her sons—2 rather nice looking 25-ish year old boys, and rattles something off in her own language—which I can only assume is "Check this chick out!—hanging onto me for dear life! Poor pet—she probably doesn't fly much!?" as they all go into fits of histerics.

Embarrassment!

But not long to go now, and we land, safely albeit laboriously, having flown over the entire city, circling and flying back into land. Somehow, however the descent does not bother me, and I feel "safe" in the knowledge that there is life below. Safely, and without drama we land. And I have (finally) let go of the little white haired lady.

(Well there was no drama apart from the fact that most of the passengers are on their feet prior to landing, clamouring to get their bags out of the overhead lockers and ensure they are the first off the plane.) Somehow (and weirdly), my nervousness at this point has subsided—well we are a few hundred feet from safety and I am already looking forward to my long weekend! I think the fact that I have used all my energy gripping the little lady and willing the plane to stay in the air, and then land safely, I am all out of energy to worry about landing.

So, I arrive at the airport in Baku and look for the taxi driver that you have sent for me. His name is Ilham.

Ilham comes bounding across to me and smiles his huge golden toothy smile (he has several gold teeth) and shouting excitedly "you Amy friend! You Amy friend!"—yup! That's me! Do I stand out that much? Apparently so.

We head to his car—not a Lada, but an unknown variety of vehicle (it probably did belong to a make and model at one time, but it has been bashed, and rusted, and chipped into a form all of its very own) and as this is my carriage for the night, it is 4 in the morning and I am tired (and also now thankfully on terra firma) I am really not caring.

I jump in and then Ilham puts on the sounds! Bless him—a collection of Scottish tunes ranging from the Proclaimers (which he sings beautifully "I'm on my way . . . from misery to happiness . . . . aha aha aha aha . . . .") He really gets into it. Manages to say "misery" with a good roll of the rrrr and clearly loves the "AHA" bits—of which there are several.

There is Deacon Blue, Hue and Cry, Texas, the theme from Brave heart and I feel all sentimental and quite definitely Scottish. Loving it.

Ilham is polite and cheery and offers me a cigarette which I politely decline and then quite randomly shouts "You fucking wanker" at the top of his voice at a Lada cutting him up on the road.

I am chortling at this and say "I see the Scottish girls are teaching you good English!" to which he replies "bloody bastards!" rolling his rrrs wonderfully.

Along the way, I notice some rather amusing footprints on the windscreen. I wonder to myself . . . . But say nothing at this point. Ilham sees me looking and points at the footprints—"Amy feet" he says. I smile.

The rest of the journey is reasonably uneventful, although I marvel (once again) at the inordinate change to the roads, buildings and architecture from the airport to Baku city that has emerged in the years since I first started visiting.

When I first visited Baku, in 1997, it was, like Aktau very much an "ex Soviet" type city with buildings that were run down and a little bit ugly. Not sure if you ever saw it like this?

But today, I am looking at new building after new building and designer shops running for over a mile whilst the boulevard that once had nothing, is now awash with lights, merry go rounds, pubs, restaurants and the "Park Bulvar" that you keep telling me about with its nine west, an Oasis and even a Debenhams! Tremendous.

So I arrive at your apartment where I have stayed before—downgraded when you moved to your current company where the budget is clearly a tad lower than previously!! But it is large and it has air conditioning so what more do we need?

A quick hug from you and off to bed.

The next morning, (all of 3 hours later) here you are screaming into my bedroom declaring "we have a new house guest and I am nae chuffed! You will hae to get rid o' it!"

(Funny that—the EX boss thing has definitely gone to your head. Who is the bossy one now?!)

I sleepily mumble "what is it?" and you say "It's a bloody lizard. She has run behind the washing machine" (located in the bathroom) "and you will hae to get her. I've left you a bowl!"

"Yeah thanks, no problem" I think and go back to sleep. (Bliss—I am not working and you have to go in to work!! Sorry, but I am secretly rather pleased about this.)

By the time I surface and go to meet you several hours later, I have forgotten about Liz (the newly nicknamed Lizard) and we head for lunch.

You however don't take long to remind me of Liz. And you tell me at this point that you have phoned your landlord to tell him the apartment is "infested" and if he doesn't remove the infestation you are moving out.

A slight over reaction don't you think?

I didn't have the heart to tell you at this point that the lizard is not only totally harmless but actually a welcome house guest as it will get rid of all the unwanted other "house guests."

But you are having none of it, and appear somewhat put out when your landlord laughs down the phone and explains that you are living in a hot country and that you need to "get over it"!!

Next port of call is your local Azeri "friend" who is still "interested" I question?! For quite some months this poor man had a rather large "crush" on you which was not lost on you, who used him unrelentlessly to bring you bacon rolls on hangover days and whatever you fancy on a whim.

He is also told that he should come and get rid of the lizard as you are quite simply petrified and don't plan on living with a salamander!

Unfortunately this doesn't work either, and it is back to me to do the deed.

You tell me that you don't mind being there whilst I am around but if it is not gone by the time I go, you are leaving too!

So on to our first evening out.

OMG—some things just never ever change. Yes, the buildings are new, and the place has been tidied up a bit, but the expats ("al' mannies" as you refer to them all) are all still there in all their glory—many of whom have a young Azeri "burrrd" on their arm—and think they are "Airchie". Hey I have no issue with guys having a good time, nor of availing themselves of the delights of Baku. Many are happily single or divorced and have every right to do as they please. For many, it is quite simply "kids in a sweetie shop" and who am I to judge? If young free and single, or old, free and divorced, I have no issue and "Good luck" to them is all I say.

I have no issue whatsoever.

I do however have a small issue with the fat, ugly, vocal ones that clearly went through some brain transplant at Baku airport and now look in the mirror and see "Mel Gibson" or "Robert Redford" looking back at them, and look down their noses on the "us UK burds". Especially, when these are the very same fat, ugly "mannies" that also have wives living back home somewhere.

I wonder if these wives are blissfully ignorant or more likely **blissfully aware** that their mannies are over here happy as "larry" or chuffed as "Airchie" and are these same wives actually secretly quite happy to be rid of them? I wonder.

And there we are—first pub of the evening, and it's like watching your life run past you in slow motion. Seriously!

A collection of people from Aberdeen, Glasgow or the "North East" (of England)—Newcastle / Middlesbrough / Sunderland and many faces I have met, worked with, worked for or worse still . . . snogged! (Ugh.)

There are people I have not seen in over 10 years and it is wonderful to reminisce back to my early career. To be remembered by my pre-married name (I am no longer married but still go by my married name) and it's great to have people remember your full birth name.

And then there are those that you simply don't want to remember or even know. The guys that have at times dampened your door because you know (thankfully they perhaps don't) that they were disciplined for "peeing on a plant" in their hotel corridor or danced naked in full glory (normally having denied it was them despite being caught on cctv) after a drunken night out.

But all in all it is all good—plenty people that I am happy to see, to have a laugh with, accept a cold beer and just say "hi" after oh so many years.

So a good night is being had, and we totter up the road (well actually Ilham comes to get us) circa 11pm—because we are having an early night! You are working tomorrow.

So, another day goes by and you are at work, and I go for a little browse around shops. Have you noticed how the shop assistants follow you around? You stop, and almost like a game of "statues" they stop. Then you move an inch, and so do they? It is slightly off putting at first. But once you get used to this shadow, you finally learn to become oblivious.

But it is rather fun to wander about the city centre, and marvel at how much Fountain Square has changed and been cleaned up over the years, and how many more buildings have been squeezed in between what existed before. The Old City is now very clean and no traffic allowed within. Very nice.

At times it can be a little off putting to wander around (Ok I am tall with blonde hair) with every single Azeri man tripping over himself as he stares (not subtley) as I walk past. New blood!

I wander about for a few hours down to the rather splendid buzzing boulevard that looks out over the Caspian. Not as clean in Baku as the clean green/ blue sparkling Caspian of Aktau but nevertheless pleasant. Again it's nice to see the enormous change. When I first visited, there was nothing here at all. Literally nothing. Now it is quite literally awash with people, street vendors, outside pubs, restaurants and of course, shopping centres.

I literally have no problem wiling away the hours until you finish work (although my decision to wear a high pair of wedge platform shoes is definitely a mistake as my feet are now killing me), and we head to the pub . . . again. I find myself back in the exact seat from the night before and it still fits—perfectly.

A few of the girls are out tonight and we get girlie chat! Brill—I've not had that in a few weeks and relish their knowledge about the "mannies" of Baku, and a couple are married to said "mannies" who, may I quickly hasten to add are part of the ex colleague group and very nice! But to you, Ames they are all "mannies".

So another good night, and another trip home with Ilham. Tonight however I get to see Betts in full flow—and as you have taken over as well and truly the boss in this partnership you sit in the front seat with your feet firmly stuck to the windscreen. Now I understand the feet marks.

I decide that we need food—and Ilham has a plan. Take us to a friend's kebab house. Great, I think. But with the one way system in Baku, we may not have gone very far, but it feels as though we have driven to Aktau as it seems to take forever. You and I are quite happy singing away to what I now discover is Ilham's only "sounds"—the Scottish tape you made for him, and together we sing loudly once again "I'm on my way from misery to happiness aha, aha aha aha . . . .". Ilham joins in and all is happy. By the time we get to the kebab shop you are lying flat out in the front seat with your feet now on the ceiling—more lovely Amy shaped paw prints on the car roof.

Another great night—thanks.

The rest of the trip all goes much the same way. Albeit I have a slightly sore head on Saturday and feel that I will never ever drink again!

But I do—after I finally get up—and make my way to a hairdresser with your pal. My first ever hairdo outside the UK and I am not quite sure what to expect. But it all goes rather well (after the initial shaking of the head in response to ability to carry out highlights), and I have made a full recovery ahead of another night out!

We have a girlie night out—and make our way to a rather posh Chinese restaurant—apparently where the President goes and the food is fantastic. We have already started the evening with a bottle of champers and are now having another.

The evening progresses and we are joined at one stage by an Azeri girl who has latched on to us and clearly thinks our chat is great.

The night all in all is quite subdued and no crazy stories to tell.

So it is Sunday and its my last day before returning to Aktau. We have a long lie and get ready for a day beside the pool.

First however, we need to go back and pick up your sunglasses—left in the pub on Thursday night. Somewhat hilariously on asking for your sunglasses, you are not only given said sunglasses but a plastic bag full of clothing items. Within the bag there is an array of goodies that range from 1 lone shoe, 2 scarves, a top (!!) a cardigan and 3 socks! I hasten to add they are not all yours as we discover but some of these items are! Excellent—we also know the culprit who owns the top! Unsure how she got home—but clearly without her top!

And then I ask to see the photos of a night out you had had there previously. Some excellent photos! But on closer examination someone has defaced your picture with a moustache (no big deal) and the words "fatty" on your forehead. I am embarrassed, but quite frankly incensed! Furious, in fact.

I play this down as I am unsure as to what you are feeling to it, but I am quite frankly annoyed for the following reasons:

1) You are absolutely not fat.
2) Even if you were fat, you are my friend, you are lovely and it would be irrelevant
3) You are are curvy and lovely (and I am outraged)
4) How could a grown adult think this in any way funny? (I am still outraged)
5) So, I want blood! Is this some fat, ugly "mannie" that thinks he is "Airchie pluff" thinking that he has any right to say that about you? I bloody hope not.

6) Or is it a jealous Azeri girl worried that you might steal one of their so called "mannies"?

We don't talk about it, but if you are not annoyed I am hurt on your behalf. It is quite simply the behaviour of a jealous adolescent! But given this is a pub—where no-one under the age of 18 (quite frankly no-one under the age of 40!) goes, then it is supposedly the actions of an adult.

Anyway, we are far too cool to let this bother us.
So, we have an afternoon at the pool to look forward to, and then I am leaving later tonight. Thanks for being a great hostess and for another great few days in Baku.

Dear Jan

Well my friend. Missing you! Still. However, you are so not going to believe this?

Things are going well and J and I have not fallen out—at all. Not even once. (Well we did have a little disagreement in the car prior to Kazakhstan when we were in Crete—I forgot the route!) But other than that, it has been bliss.

I am back in Kazakhstan after a few days in Baku, Azerbaijan where things never change!

You are so not going to believe what an evening "out" entails for us. Yes, I fully accept that J has been based in Kazakhstan for over 7 years now, and he has pretty much tried all the places he considers to be "good" places to eat. But nevertheless an evening out does not mean going anywhere other than out the balcony door and on to our 13th floor (yes it is massive) balcony! And the weather is warm and lovely—but that is really taking "going out" to a whole new dimension.

All that is needed for our night in "out" on the balcony is:

1) Various alcoholic beverages
2) A few nibbles
3) 1 Laptop

Our internet connection works well and we can take the laptop outside (no neither of us have got i-pods) and avail ourselves of a little bit of music via You Tube.

We start with a gin and tonic and often move on to a little sophisticated bottle of vino before cranking up the You tube and banging on the tunes!

The general evening starts off quite sedately, and we normally put on some easy listening or a few tracks in the current charts.

As the evening wears on and we have moved from the aperitif drinks of gin and tonics, through a bottle of wine and perhaps moving on to vodka, the evening ramps up nicely. This is the point at which we start to take it in turns to choose our own You tube video and tune and this can be quite amusing.

Our taste in music varies dramatically primarily due to the fact that his era was basically in the 70s and I was very much an 80s teenager.

J's choices are varied and can be everything from The Moody Blues, Miles Davis, Lou Armstrong and Neil Young, my choices are normally such wonders as Kajagoogoo (pictures of Limahl used to plaster my teenage bedroom walls), Nik Kershaw, Spandau Ballet and Duran Duran and often I have to indulge myself in a lot of Wham! J is generally and always bored if not horrified at the amount of George Michael I can subject him to in any one given evening—as it turns out I have remained a stalwart and very long term fan. (I was the one of my group of friends that thought George Michael was far more handsome than Andrew Ridgeley and despite the revelation that George was, in fact gay—never perturbed me from my long standing love affair with his music.)

Our style in music is indeed different, but over the course of this summer we have acquainted eachother with quite a wide array of musical taste and genius.

What has become the theme of the evening, however is as we progress further on into the night, we then remember our childhood (or mine rather) and following my memories of my parents, I remind J of all my parents singles and albums.

We had to bang on the Seekers—having just remembered all about them, and Julie Felix (going to the Zoo). Going to the Zoo now is a regular event on an evening "in" and we are completely up to speed on all the words!

Throughout the summer we have also reminded ourselves of all our favourite childhood programmes and these include "Mary Mungo and Midge", "Chigley" "Trumpton", "Bagpuss", "Play School", "Ivor the Engine"—(that is a particular favourite of mine—I put on my best Welsh accent at this time and seem to repeat over and over—depending on how much gin as been consumed "Ivor and the Draaagon".

But the piece de resistance.
The highlight of the night.
The final part of the evening—and it works every time—is a little bit of Play Away.

J is quite literally amazed at the legend of Brian Cant and his ability to make us return to our childhood selves.

I kid you not, Brian Cant is a legend. Of the highest order.

We have mastered the "Court of King Caracticus." It goes something like this . . ." The scintillating witches that put the stitches in the britches of the boys that put the powder on the noses of the faces of the ladies of the harem of the court of King Caracticus . . . was just passing by . . ." (repeated several times over and over again) there are a bunch of great actions to go with this masterpiece of childhood delights and boy are we getting into it. Hilarious.

We finish up the evening with the title tune to "Play away" as Brian Cant sings his heart out and Jeremy Irons (honest to god—THE Jeremy Irons started his career on Play away OMG!) is sitting there playing the guitar and also crooning away to "Play away way away way, away away way away!!."

J and I always finish up the evening dancing around our large dining room singing away to Play Away!

Dear Loops

Well I have met some expat "wives". I have been here almost 5 weeks and been quite happy to spend my weeks doing a little bit of work, plenty of sunbathing on the balcony and managing to go to the gym 3 or 4 times a week.

The gym at the Renaissance hotel is fantastic and rarely has more than a couple of people in it at once.

To be honest, it is really quite bizarre I am rather enjoying my own company! Yup—all day long on my own with evenings being a sort of "wife." Don't get me wrong, I have not taken to doing the cooking—that is a step beyond the duties, but I do manage to do the washing and the washing up! That's about it really as we have a cleaner to wash the floors, clean the bathrooms, do the ironing and anything else that might be necessary.

So I have met a few other expat wives now, and have been invited to their lunches! They meet twice a week—Tuesdays and Thursdays, and as I am working from home 3 days I decide that I will join them on a Thursday.

I am quite excited. Some real girl chat and perhaps the chance to avail myself of a little liquid lunching. Any excuse to have a cheeky wee glass of vino sounds good to me!

So my first lunch, I arrive in style—J allows his driver to return to Aktau early and drive me to "Coffee and People" where I meet a mixture of ladies from the US, Canada, Argentina, the Philippines and Ireland for a little light lunch.

I am, however, ever so slightly disappointed when I arrive 5 minutes late to discover that all round the table are bottles of water! I am hoping at this point that this is simply the starter and a means to keep hydrated in the sunshine.

For me a lunchtime is a luxury. In all my career driven working, I have rarely if ever even managed to get a lunch apart from a quick bite at my desk, and therefore an opportunity to eat out at lunchtime, and not have to rush back to work, is an occasion to be treasured, enjoyed and MUST include a glass of wine—or a wee champers on a special occasion.

But alas no!
It appears that these ladies are water drinkers. And I am not only disappointed but actually slightly horrified. It seems a little bit of a waste of being an expat wife if one cannot partake of a little light lunch libation of the alcoholic variety—does it not?

But nevertheless I feel that it would be slightly rude to suggest on my first invite to order a glass of wine. So water is the extent of our libation this lunchtime and no afternoon of vino is to transpire.

The chat is good, and the ladies are lovely. Albeit an eclectic mix that you can't help wondering would ever really be friends if it wasn't for the fact that the only thing we all have in common is accompanying our partners / husbands in Aktau. The age range is circa 30 years! But I like the extreme mix of nationalities, experiences, careers, and interests and it is another new and fun experience to add to the mix.

Dear Dad

Well today I am off to get some outside lights for the party that we are having this weekend.

Shouldn't be too difficult, should it? I have Gena, our driver to do the driving, the speaking and the paying, so not much for me to do but choose the lights. Easy!

So we arrive at the "light" shop and enter.

On first sight it is quite modern looking and there is quite a spectacular array of light fittings, drills, light switches, outside wiring boxes—everything you could need for an outside area. The light fittings display was huge and varied from lanterns to half moon fittings and plenty "round ball" type light fittings in every shape and size imagineable.

I am impressed, and relieved.

So, after no more than 2 minutes, Gena and I have chosen 4 light fittings that we both like (and that we know J will like as he has been specific about the basic style of the fitting):

The shop is full of "assistants" but unsurprisingly (I really shouldn't be surprised after having been here a while) but I remain surprised that there is no-one rushing to our aid! We stand for another 10 minutes (well we are not in a hurry) and I say to Genadi—"is anyone actually going to serve us?") He shrugs his shoulder and laughs and then slopes off to find someone to serve us. He returns with someone perched behind a counter in the next "room" and a very smiley nice assistant, if not slightly disinterested, and clearly with no sense of urgency follows us back so we can point out our desired light fittings.

Excellent.

So, we point to choice number 1. She shakes her head and than rattles something off in Russian. Gena turns to me and translates:

"The don't have this."
"Oh joy!" I think
But not to worry, we have another 3 choices, all of which will look splendid on our balcony so I point to choice number 2.
Our smiling but lazy assistant, again shakes her head and says something else.
This time, the translation is "This is not for sale."
"What do you mean this is not for sale?" I wonder, but still unperturbed I point to choice no. 3.
Nope—another shake of the head and I ask "Is this not for sale either?" to which the translation is "No, this is not for sale."
This time, I want a little more explanation because I am wondering why it is not for sale and ask Genadi "What do you mean?"
Another exchange in Russian and a bit of shaking of heads and the translation turns out to be "We don't stock it."

"What do you mean you don't stock it?" I say

To this, I say to Genadi "Why the hell are they displaying items they don't stock?"

Gena translates my question (I suspect without adding in the expletive) and the response is a simple shrug of the shoulders. (This I understand without any translation.)

I think her look said something along the lines of this:

"I don't really care why it is not in stock. It is not in stock. And **YOU** can't buy it. So just get over it. And besides, if we only displayed the things we actually have, the shop would be empty!"

I realise at this point that our starting question should have been "what do you sell?" but as we only have one preferred item left, I carry on down the path we started and point to our fourth and final choice (well, I am NOT having Chinese lanterns or patterned gawdy looking outside lights in my balcony. No sureee.) I am sure that there will be another shake of the head, and off we will have to go to several other light shops, most probably placed in several different micro districts across the city, taking up most of the rest of the afternoon. I am almost resigned to my fate, when the assistant nods her head (albeit slowly.)

"Hoorah" I shout inside my head. Ordinarily, I would be pretty friggin' annoyed at the lack of service, the total disinterest, the fact that stock is displayed that is not for sale, and the minutes of my precious life that are being wasted away in this slowly becoming very uninteresting shop! However, I am not annoyed.

I am really actually rather relieved (must have been in Kaz a while now) that we may get a decent light fitting **and** in the first shop we try!

So our assistant disappears to get the items. Or that is what I assume she is doing. We wait. And we wait. And we wait a little longer.

I am beginning to wonder if she has "gone to lunch" like one of our previous shopping excursions but just hasn't bothered to tell us.

By this time, Gena and I are starting to act like a couple of school children (well our attention spans are being sorely tried) and we have started playing "cowboys and Indians" with the drills—which come in every shape and size available. We are hiding at either side of the aisle and shooting each other! How mature!

Nobody seems to care though. In fact I am not even sure if they have noticed!

But it takes care of the further 10 minutes (I kid you not) that it takes for our assistant to locate the 4 light fittings we have requested.

So, I think we are almost ready to go, but really, I should know better than this.

The next part of the process is to take each and every fitting out of its box, unscrew it, look inside it, check for . . . . I have no idea what?, scratches?, chips? (who knows—they are made of plastic and fairly impenetrable) but check each and every one out—we do. (I should remember this from the 2 previous occasions buying light fittings for inside.)

And then . . . . and I love this bit! We are choosing the light bulbs! Honestly—please let's just grab 4 light bulbs and make haste! Nope, several different light bulbs come out of their boxes and are then put into a little contraption that lights them up. Great, they work!

Having gone through this to choose the size, the shape and the wattage of the bulb I point and nod and say "that one will do". However, that is not good enough, they want to be sure that "that one will not only do" but that it is perfect in every way possible and then each light bulb has to be put into the actual light fitting, compared with each light bulb against another and then tested inside one of the new light fittings! It is a thorough process! But my head is literally screaming "THAT ONE WILL DO!!!!!!!"

We choose the preferred wattage and Genadi orders 8 bulbs (good idea I think—we will need more bulbs at some point) and then I wish he had only chosen the required 4 because, true to form, each and ever single light bulb comes out of its box, out of its packaging and is TESTED—to make sure it works!! Could you imagine being in B and Q, being at the check out queue and having every item within your trolley unpackaged and checked, unscrewed, unpackaged, re-packaged, tested . . . . Whilst a queue of irate Brits are queueing up in long lines behind? (Not to mention that each item has to be written out, by hand on an individual bill (NO bar codes), taken to the cashier (elsewhere), stamped and paid before returning to collect the goods!!!!!)

I believe this is all a throw-back to the Soviet days when nothing worked and had to be checked. But "OMG"—how long do we have to spend in this shop?

Then, light bulbs all tested, the assistant starts the process of repackaging each and every light bulb up, and goes to screw each light fitting back together!

"NO!!!!" my internal voice is shouting, and remembering back to a similar experience that J had recounted when choosing light switches some months back, I get very serious, and with an extremely serious look on my face I grab a plastic bag!

I then very boldly lean over the counter (this just goes to show what happens to a normally calm sane expat individual after almost an hour in a light fitting shop playing cowboys and Indians) wrap my whole arm from shoulder to hand around all the items on the counter—of which there are a fair number and sweep them in one clean and concise movement, quickly and without fuss into the plastic bag!!!

The assistant (and I think most of the other people in the shop) are slightly shocked and look a little stunned by my total disrespect for the process, as several people stop talking and stare.

But for me, this shop is history!—I am done, and we are going!!
Well, there really is only so much time that any woman should
have to spend in an "outside light fitting" shop!

So I go—out the door and leave Genadi trailing behind me
probably having to explain away my actions. Bless him again.

Anyway, the good news is that the light fittings are now fitted
and look excellent. J loves them and we are all set for our party!

Dear Bro

Well we do have a huge TV, with surround sound, 2 dvd players and SKY! Sounds excellent doesn't it?

J has always maintained that with the football season fast approaching that his winter days and nights are spent watching endless premiership football and what's more he is able to access all the latest movies!

I have been happy and excited about this for some time. Not so much the football, which I can tolerate from time to time. (Well I can more than tolerate a bit of Manchester United being a stalwart fan, but anything else I can take or leave.)

Anyway, don't let him fool you. The Sky is extremely (and I mean EXTREMELY) temperamental! On moving into the apartment I was assured that the "TV and Internet man"—a very affable and fluent English speaking Russian has set up our internet (which incidentally works perfectly) and the satellite television, and we are going to be in for a treat of any and all sport we can possibly wish to watch, any amount of sci-fi, CSI and NCIS (I just love all the US crime fiction programmes) and as many movies as we can possibly want to watch.

So it all sounded rather promising—several weeks ago!

But since we moved in, we have had to have our Russian TV man over 3 times and he is now avoiding J's phone calls! Bless him.

We are regularly sitting watching some television programme and the screen simply freezes. Or J goes onto the menu to check out what is on, and within seconds of touching a few buttons we have lost connection to the whole lot!! A whole column of zeros—and nothing on the TV!

(This is the point when I can hear J shouting any number of flowery expletives and regardless of the room I am, I normally just shout back "TV OFF?")

I have decided the best ploy is to keep firmly away from all the remote controls, firm in the knowledge that if I don't touch them I can't be blamed for anything going wrong.

But go wrong it does—pretty regularly.

I am told that the problem is something along the following lines:

There is a man in Croatia and a man somewhere else that control our Sky connection which, apparently is accessed through the internet. Apparently, one or other of them sometimes simply forgets to pay the subscription and so we get no television. Sounds like an excellent set up!!

Anyway, thank goodness it is summer and I can avail myself of the balcony, watch the sunsets and watch the troops of cars zooming by. (Every time there is a wedding, processions of cars scoot down the road with their hands firmly placed on and pressing the horns loudly!) Who needs the TV anyway?

Dear D
(my ex colleague and stalwart chomping mate)

I have just been souvenir shopping for my return to blighty! Not much to buy thankfully so I have availed myself of several rather cute brightly dressed camels! Well camels are rife here and they are quite cute.

I have bought a rather large camel for Toots number 1 (my gorgeous niece) and several other smaller versions of the same thing. 1 of these little camels is most definitely for Toots number 2—your lovely daughter who I am looking forward to seeing and reading a few stories to. Not sure what she will make of said camel—but I hope she will realise that it is given with much love!

Apart from that I have not much else to show for my 12 weeks in this rather interesting but crazy place. A few miniature bottles of vodka and a book for my Dad!

See you soon!

Dear Ms French (Dawn)
(of French and Saunders fame)

I am writing to you not because I know you, not because we have ever met, not because before this summer I really considered you in anyway "special" or different from many of the British comic treasures that us Brits have. No, not for any of those reasons. (That is not to say that I don't find you funny, you understand. No, indeed. French and Saunders was a "stapler" for me in British comedy growing up—and the spin off series—yes I know this was the "brain child" of your partner in crime, Jennifer—Absolutely Fabulous is, quite frankly one of my favourite programmes of all time.)

But no, I don't write to you for that reason.

Nor is it likely that we will ever have that pleasure to meet—(although I suspect the pleasure would sit quite firmly at my door as for you, I suspect meeting me would not be as, well, fortuitous, exciting or wonderful experience—given that you met the Queen Mother aka "Spam" when you were 4 years old.)

Don't get me wrong, if we do EVER have the pleasure of meeting I will remember a few key points of my own (and like you prior to meeting the QM, I will happily practice for days and weeks beforehand):

1) I won't bow or curtsy (you clearly have the monopoly on that having practiced for weeks prior to meeting HRH the QM)—and I don't think that you strictly count as royalty although should you wish a curtsy I can happily oblige
2) I will be extremely polite and try not to be too funny

3) I will not be over zealous and come eagerly up to you autograph book in hand when you are enjoying a family day out—I know that's a "no no"
4) I will absolutely NOT announce your arrival at my house over a tannoy system or, in fact tell anyone that you are coming (oh apart maybe from my bezzie, Janice as we might want to include her in our little chat.)

No, should we ever meet, I will wait for you to come and speak to me at which point I will be most delighted to speak to you, have a cup of tea and try not to look too awestruck.

The reason I am writing to you is because you have, (yes I know you don't know this) have played a really rather large part in my life this summer.

I have read 2 of your books (don't know at this point whether or not you have written any others) but the 2 books—" Dear Fatty "and "A little bit marvellous", the latter of which was given to me by my "bezzie" prior to this ¼ of a year assignment to deepest Asia, have quite literally changed my life.

(Actually, maybe if we do ever meet you can bring Jennifer (Saunders) along too and then I could bring my bezzie, Janice and we could chat away like old friends and perhaps find that the 2 partnerships are quite frankly very similar. Not, I admit, that Janice and I have the comic genius nor the renown and celebrity of you and Jen, but in the comfort of our little (thankfully unknown) lives in Aberdeen, we have many a story that could provide you with some startling material on which to base your sketches. (Perhaps we might need a glass of wine to get into those.) Janice and I would also look rather good in a Madonna suit!

Anyway, I typically digress.

I write to you with Thanks.

You have kept me smiling and laughing away for much of the summer—in between my crazy, frustrating, often long but rarely dull Aktau shopping experiences whilst I lay on the balcony in the sunshine book in hand.

You, are quite frankly a genius, and I really have to tell you that whilst reading "Dear Fatty" I was quite literally wetting myself as I read about your equestrian prowess, aged what I think may have been circa 12 atop Shula, your little bald pony with a disease called "sweet itch" (which sounded to me like some horsey version of thrush but thankfully was not), clad in, and I quote from your book "my dad's old gardening jackets and my welly boots" "wobbling about on a scuffed old saddle atop a scabby, bald, fat pony". By the time I got to the part where Shula was farting her way during your gymkhana (amidst some posher girls on posher ponies with posher outfits) and you describe the humiliation of being on the saddle "which had never fitted properly and which had gradually worked its way up to Shula's shoulders where it was utterly loose, just slid slowly all the way round, with me (you) still attached." and then went on to say "For a brief second before I hit the grass I was actually riding my pony upside down", I had tears rolling down my face, as I am lying in bed with poor J wondering what on earth I am reading! J then made me read the whole passage back to him and the pair of us are lying there in bed, in Aktau, Kazakhstan in fits of histerics!

Dawn (can I call you that?)—Thank you. You are hilarious and you have kept me chortling all summer—even amidst the bizarre crazy frustrations that have come along with living in an ex Soviet culture that really has no concept of customer service.

And what's more, you have helped inspire me to do some writing too—and for that I have to acknowledge your "help" in bringing this book to fruition.

So, if we do meet, then I hope you will accept a cup of tea and a bit of cake (made by my Mum not me because I don't cook), or a coffee, or a juice, or should you prefer something stronger than I can offer a beer (of whichever variety you like), or a cider, or a glass of wine (red or white you can choose), or a glass of champagne (or a bottle should you wish), or a mojito, or a bellini, or a cosmopolitan or a whisky, gin, vodka, martini (dry, sweet, medium) or whatever tipple you would like as the drinks are on me!

Thank you

Dear Jan

Well my summer is almost over and I will be heading back to Aberdeen in a couple of days.

I really can't quite believe how fast it has all passed by and how incredibly well I have taken to this whole experience!

I guess if I was to summarise the experience it would have to be:

1) Hot! I love the sun (it has been sunny more or less every day and I have enjoyed a real long proper summer. Even the rain only lasts a couple of hours!)
2) Hot! I love the balcony
3) Hot! Love J (sorry had to say that!)
4) Love the apartment
5) Love the shopping excursions with Genadi to furnish the apartment—customer service has yet to make its way to Aktau!

I am looking bonny and brown if not a few pounds heavier than when I started.

What have I missed?:

1) You!
2) The rest of my friends and family—sometimes.
3) Fish and chips
4) Shopping for boots! (and other clothes)
5) Lettuce (OK—I was able to get lettuce occasionally but never ever was able to get it in the supermarket)
6) Houmous!
7) My sis in law to take care of my "roots!"

The family that have moved into the unfinished concrete shell at the foot of our building next door (presumably living there illegally) are going to have a very long and cold winter. And J and I have been discussing all summer how they will survive the cold without some serious winter woollies. So J and I have done a clearout of all his unused jumpers, sweatshirts, sweatpants and thick winter site jackets and thrown them over the wall.

Can't wait to see you!

P.S. I have written to Dawn French and hope we might get to meet her one day! I thought we might offer to body double for them in Madonna suits!

PPS Get the champagne chilling I will be home soon!

PPPS Just before we left we were able to see that our next door neighbours have made good use of their *new* clothes and they are all hanging up on the washing line! Fantastic. We have left our mark and they will be warm! (We threw in a few tins of tuna fish, beans and sweetcorn too!)

Bibliography

Dear Fatty by Dawn French (2008)
Published 2009, Arrow Books

About the Author

Tracy S Smith was born and brought up in Aberdeen, Scotland and has an honours degree in Psychology. By day she is normally, and formally an HR professional (most of the time) who has travelled extensively within her Oil and Gas related career! Her work over the years has allowed her the great opportunity to travel to many great places including Kazakhstan.

The summer of 2011 brought about a whole new experience! Living, not business visiting Aktau, Kazakhstan brought a wealth of new fun that could never be experienced on a business trip.

This book is a must read for anyone who enjoys travelling, likes different cultures and above all, has a sense of humour.

Lightning Source UK Ltd.
Milton Keynes UK
UKOW052341270112

186189UK00001B/14/P